Math Mammoth
Grade 6
Skills Review Workbook

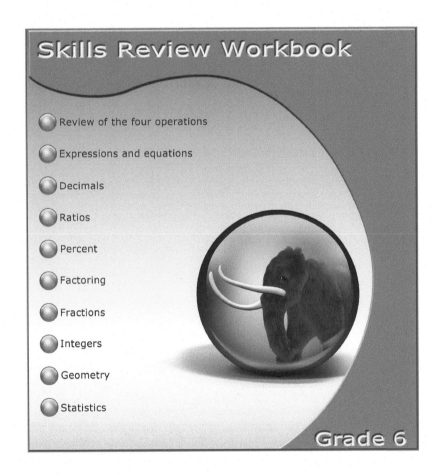

By Maria Miller

Contents

Foreword 6

Chapter 1: Review of the Basic Operations
Skills Review 1 7
Skills Review 2 8
Skills Review 3 9
Skills Review 4 10

Chapter 2: Expressions and Equations
Skills Review 5 11
Skills Review 6 12
Skills Review 7 13
Skills Review 8 14
Skills Review 9 15
Skills Review 10 16
Skills Review 11 17
Skills Review 12 18
Skills Review 13 19

Chapter 3: Decimals
Skills Review 14 20
Skills Review 15 21
Skills Review 16 22
Skills Review 17 23
Skills Review 18 24
Skills Review 19 25
Skills Review 20 26
Skills Review 21 27
Skills Review 22 28
Skills Review 23 29
Skills Review 24 30
Skills Review 25 31
Skills Review 26 32
Skills Review 27 33

Chapter 4: Ratios

Skills Review 28 34

Skills Review 29 35

Skills Review 30 36

Skills Review 31 37

Skills Review 32 38

Skills Review 33 39

Skills Review 34 40

Chapter 5: Percent

Skills Review 35 41

Skills Review 36 42

Skills Review 37 43

Skills Review 38 44

Skills Review 39 45

Skills Review 40 46

Skills Review 41 47

Chapter 6: Prime Factorization, GCF, and LCM

Skills Review 42 48

Skills Review 43 49

Skills Review 44 50

Skills Review 45 51

Skills Review 46 52

Chapter 7: Fractions

Skills Review 47 53

Skills Review 48 54

Skills Review 49 55

Skills Review 50 56

Skills Review 51 57

Skills Review 52 58

Skills Review 53 59

Skills Review 54 60

Chapter 8: Integers

Skills Review 55 61

Skills Review 56 62

Skills Review 57 63

Skills Review 58 64

Skills Review 59 65

Skills Review 60 66

Skills Review 61 67

Chapter 9: Geometry

Skills Review 62 68

Skills Review 63 69

Skills Review 64 70

Skills Review 65 71

Skills Review 66 72

Skills Review 67 74

Skills Review 68 76

Skills Review 69 78

Skills Review 70 79

Skills Review 71 80

Skills Review 72 82

Skills Review 73 84

Chapter 10: Statistics

Skills Review 74 86

Skills Review 75 88

Skills Review 76 90

Skills Review 77 92

Skills Review 78 93

Skills Review 79 95

Skills Review 80 97

Foreword

Math Mammoth Grade 6 Skills Review Workbook has been created to complement the lessons in *Math Mammoth Grade 6* complete curriculum. It gives the students practice in reviewing what they have already studied, so the concepts and skills will become more established in their memory.

These review worksheets are designed to provide a spiral review of the concepts in the curriculum. This means that after a concept or skill has been studied in the main curriculum, it is then reviewed repeatedly over time in several different worksheets of this book.

This book is divided into chapters, according to the corresponding chapters in the *Math Mammoth Grade 6* curriculum. You can choose exactly when to use the worksheets within the chapter, and how many of them to use. Not all students need all of these worksheets to help them keep their math skills fresh, so please vary the amount of worksheets you assign your student(s) according to their needs.

Most of the worksheets are designed to be one page, and include a variety of exercises in a fun way without becoming too long and tedious.

The printed answer key can be purchased separately, or in the digital download version it is included in the zip file.

I wish you success in teaching math!

Maria Miller, the author

Skills Review 1

1. Rewrite the expressions using an exponent, then solve them. You may use a calculator.

   a. $7 \times 7 \times 7 \times 7 \times 7 \times 7$

   b. $9 \times 9 \times 9 \times 9$

   c. 80 squared

   d. 60 cubed

2. Divide. There may be a remainder. You can build a multiplication table for the divisor to help you. Lastly, check your result.

$2 \times 39 = 78$	$39\overline{)9\ 4\ 2\ 0\ 6}$	$\times\ \ 3\ \ 9$

3. Greenville High School has 5,928 students. One-eighth of the students walk or ride bikes to school, two-thirds ride the bus, and the rest ride to school in cars. What fraction of the students ride to school in cars?

4. Solve. Remember the order of operations!

   a. $5,240 - (80 + 60) \times 30 =$

   b. $325 \times 3 + \dfrac{7,200}{90} =$

5. Factor this number to its prime factors.

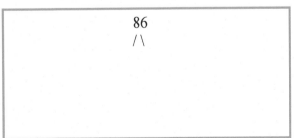

6. Complete. Note that the operation used is not always the same.

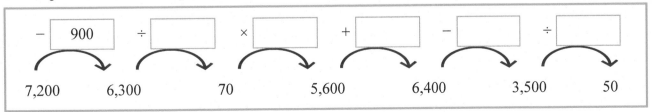

Skills Review 2

1. **a.** A train is traveling at 72 miles per hour. Fill in the table:

Miles				72 mi			
Time	10 min	20 min	30 min	1 hour	2 hours	2 ½ hours	3 hours

   b. If the train travels steadily at 72 miles per hour, how far will it travel in 8 hours?

   c. *Estimate* how many *hours* it takes the train to travel 465 miles.

2. Divide. Think: how many times does the divisor go into the dividend?

a. $3.2 \div 0.8 =$ _____	**c.** $0.21 \div 0.03 =$ _____	**e.** $6.3 \div 0.7 =$ _____
b. $0.54 \div 0.06 =$ _____	**d.** $0.015 \div 0.005 =$ _____	**f.** $4.8 \div 0.04 =$ _____

3. Find the missing numbers. The sum of any two adjacent (side-by-side) numbers is the number directly above them.

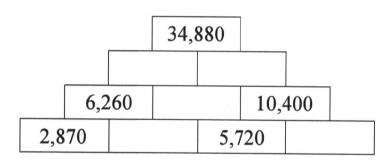

4. Multiply.

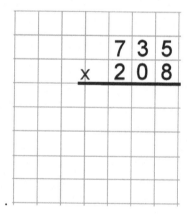

5. Susan bought two gallons of juice. She drank one cup, and then poured the rest into 12 oz bottles. How many *full* bottles of juice did she get?

6. Write in normal form (as a number).

a. $4 \times 10^3 + 7 \times 10^6 + 2 \times 10^0$	**b.** $8 \times 10^5 + 3 \times 10^7 + 9 \times 10^2 + 5 \times 10^4$

Skills Review 3

1. Round to the nearest...

Number	514,372	827,491	36,594,136	7,091,512	4,978,627
...thousand					
...ten thousand					
...hundred thousand					
...million					

2. Compare and write $<$, $>$, or $=$.

a. ten million ☐ 10^7

b. 39,000 ☐ 10^5

c. 10^8 ☐ a billion

d. $10^7 - 1000$ ☐ 10^6

e. $10^5 + 10^3$ ☐ 10^8

f. $3 \cdot 10^4$ ☐ 4×10^3

3. Fill in the pattern using a calculator.

$8^1 =$

$8^2 =$

$8^3 =$

$8^4 =$

$8^5 =$

$8^6 =$

4. Divide. Below each division, check your result.

a. $57 \div 9 =$ _____ R _____

____ · ____ + ____ = _____

b. $71 \div 6 =$ _____ R _____

____ · ____ + ____ = _____

5. Express the area (A) as a multiplication, and solve.

a. A square with a side of 8 kilometers:

A = _____

b. A square with sides 11 m long:

A = _____

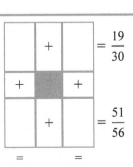

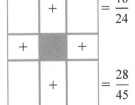

Puzzle Corner

Find the fractions that can go into the puzzles.

Hint: If the answer has a denominator of 24, think what the denominators of the two fractions could have been.

Skills Review 4

1. Estimate the result using mental math and rounded numbers. Find the exact value using a calculator. Also, find the error of estimation. In **b.**, round the exact value to two decimal digits.

a. 3,580 · 21,040	**b.** 48,732 ÷ 4,216
Estimation:	Estimation:
Exact:	Exact:
Error of estimation:	Error of estimation:

2. A certain type of fabric costs $7.45 a yard, and another costs 3/5 as much. Brenna has $90. Find out how much Brenna pays if she buys four yards of the more expensive fabric and seven yards of the cheaper fabric.

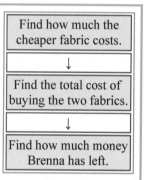

   How much money does Brenna have
   left after buying the fabric?

3. Divide. Remember that division can be written using a fraction line as well.

   a. $\dfrac{280}{7} =$ **b.** $\dfrac{96}{12} =$ **c.** $\dfrac{3500}{10} =$ **d.** $\dfrac{760}{20} =$ **e.** $\dfrac{800}{50} =$

4. Find the value of these expressions, using paper and pencil methods. Use your notebook for more space.

   a. $360 - 7.8 \times 34.2$

   b. $896 \div (18.6 + 13.4) - 19.3$

5. Find the missing factors.

a. 0.8 · _____ = 0.72	**b.** 11 · _____ = 9.9	**c.** 0.6 · _____ = 4.2

Skills Review 5

1. Write the measurements in the metric unit charts.

a. 5.46 km

km	hm	dam	m	dm	cm	mm

b. 39.8 dm

km	hm	dam	m	dm	cm	mm

c. Use the chart to do these conversions:

5.46 km = _____ hm = _____ dam = _____ m

39.8 dm = _____ m = _____ dam = _____ hm

2. Rewrite each expression using the fraction line, then solve. *Hint: Only whatever comes right after the ÷ sign needs to be in the denominator.*

a. $56 \div 7 \cdot 6$	**b.** $81 \div (9 \cdot 3) \cdot 12$	**c.** $6 \cdot 8 \div 4 \cdot 5$

3. A building has three rooms. The dimensions of the rooms are 22 ft by 12 ft, 10 ft by 12 ft, and 12 ft by 12 ft. What is the total area of the building?

4. Express the volume (V) as a multiplication, and solve.

a. A cube with edges 7 cm in length:	**b.** A cube with edges that are all 4 m long:
V = _____	V = _____

5. First convert the fractional parts into like fractions. Then add or subtract.

a. $7\frac{4}{9} - 2\frac{6}{15}$	**b.** $9\frac{7}{12} + 14\frac{3}{8}$

Skills Review 6

1. Find a number that fits in place of the unknown.

a. $x \div 80 = 70$
b. $30 \cdot M = 2{,}700$

2. Fill in the missing numbers in these equivalent fractions and mixed numbers.

a. $3\dfrac{6}{9} = 3\dfrac{2}{\square}$	**b.** $\dfrac{6}{10} = \dfrac{\square}{60}$
c. $\dfrac{4}{5} = \dfrac{12}{\square}$	**d.** $4\dfrac{1}{4} = \square\dfrac{7}{\square}$

3. Continue the patterns for six more numbers.

   a. 2,780,000; 2,820,000; 2,860,000;

   b. 923,752; 923,452; 923,152;

4. Multiply.

$$\begin{array}{r} \$\,6\;5\,.\,3\;8 \\ \times\qquad 4\;7 \\ \hline \end{array}$$

5. From the top, find your way through the maze by coloring factors of 84. You can move right, left, down, or diagonally down.

9	14	13	16
42	44	32	27
12	18	41	22
5	21	11	17
15	7	8	26
36	28	40	33
24	10	3	29

6. During a five-day workweek, Mia receives *about* 90 e-mails per day, Damian receives 2/3 as many as Mia, and Stella receives 3/4 as many as Damian.

   a. *About* how many e-mails do they receive in three weeks?

   b. If they work 49 weeks in a year, *about* how many e-mails do they receive during that time?

7. Divide in parts, then add or subtract the results.

a. $\dfrac{480 + 64}{8}$	**b.** $\dfrac{540 + 60 - 18}{6}$	**c.** $\dfrac{160 - 70}{5}$

Skills Review 7

1. Evaluate the expressions when the value of the variable is given.

a. $3x + 26$ when $x = 9$	**b.** $\dfrac{32}{z} \cdot 15$ when $z = 8$

2. Solve. Use a notebook if necessary. Also, a flowchart showing the steps of the solution may help.

Mariah bought three lamps for $42 each that had been discounted by 1/3 of their price. Shelly bought three lamps for $45 each that had been discounted by 2/5 of their price.

a. Find the original prices of the two different kinds of lamps.

b. Who saved more money overall?

How much more?

3. It costs $57 an hour to rent a personal watercraft. Kyle rents one for three hours twice a month. *Estimate* how much he will spend on rental fees in a year.

4. Divide. Check your answer by multiplying.

a. $44\overline{)9\ 5\ 4\ 8}$	$\times$ _____	**b.** $60\overline{)2\ 6\ .2\ 8}$	$\times$ _____

Skills Review 8

1. **a.** The area of a square is 81 cm^2. What is its perimeter?

   b. The volume of a cube is 125 cubic inches. How long is its (one) edge?

2. Multiply. You can use estimation to check if your answers are reasonable.

a. $3\frac{1}{4} \cdot 1\frac{4}{5}$	**b.** $1\frac{3}{5} \cdot 3\frac{1}{3}$

3. Write an expression for the illustration, and simplify it.

a. x x and x

b. z 5 z and   13

4. Match each problem with the term that correctly identifies the number(s) that are underlined.

$250 \div 50 = \underline{\mathbf{5}}$	sum
$\underline{\mathbf{32}} - 17 = 15$	divisor
$\underline{\mathbf{70}} \cdot \underline{\mathbf{8}} = 560$	minuend
$23 + 67 = \underline{\mathbf{90}}$	product
$56 - \underline{\mathbf{39}} = 17$	addends
$30 \cdot 80 = \underline{\mathbf{2400}}$	subtrahend
$\underline{\mathbf{70}} \div 5 = 14$	quotient
$\underline{\mathbf{28}} + \underline{\mathbf{35}} = 63$	difference
$81 - 23 = \underline{\mathbf{58}}$	dividend
$108 \div \underline{\mathbf{12}} = 9$	factors

5. Solve using mental math.

a. $40 \cdot 70 - 20 \cdot 60$

=

b. $800 \div 5 - 300 \div 10$

=

c. $58 + 73 + 96$

=

d. $300 \div 6 \cdot 400 \div 8$

=

Skills Review 9

1. Write an expression for each situation.

   a. 18 more than y

   b. the value, in cents, of p dimes

   c. the total number of people in 7 teams of x

2. Find the value of these expressions.

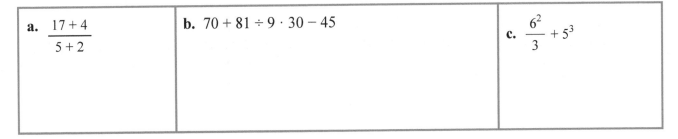

a. $\dfrac{17 + 4}{5 + 2}$	**b.** $70 + 81 \div 9 \cdot 30 - 45$	**c.** $\dfrac{6^2}{3} + 5^3$

3. Solve the decimal divisions to the asked accuracy. Use a notebook for long divisions.

   a. $77 \div 0.3$, to two decimal digits

   b $0.52 \div 0.009$, to three decimal digits

4. Write in order from the smallest to the largest.

a. 180,000,000 10^8 8,000,000,000	**b.** $3 \cdot 10^9$ $5 \cdot 10^7$ 350,000,000

5. Brandon bought a video camera for $227.99, a tripod for $175.99, and two memory cards for $25 each. Estimate the total cost.

   What was the exact cost?

6. Write each given product using subtraction or addition. Then solve using partial products.

a. $8 \cdot 397 = 8 \cdot ($ _____ $-$ _____ $)$ $=$	**b.** $6 \cdot 7,050$

Skills Review 10

1. Multiply using the distributive property.

a. $8(30 + 7) = 8 \cdot \underline{} + 8 \cdot \underline{} =$	**b.** $5(s + 9) =$
c. $z(50 + x) =$	**d.** $7(3a + 6b) =$

2. Use the clues to find sets of increasing *consecutive* numbers. All numbers used are less than 50.

   a.
   $\underline{} < \underline{} < \underline{} < \underline{}$

       prime   multiple of 7   factor of 45   square number

   b.
   $\underline{} < \underline{} < \underline{} < \underline{}$

       cube number   multiple of 4   prime   factor of 120

3. Write an expression for each scenario.

   a. The difference of x and 230, multiplied by 50.

   b. The sum of 84 and x divided by 9.

   c. The quotient of 300 and 60, subtracted from y.

4. At Bianca's Gourmet Bakery, a 9-inch lemon cheesecake costs $42, and an 8-inch apple pie costs 2/3 as much. A company bought two cheesecakes and three pies to serve at a business meeting. What was the total cost?

5. Write an expression for both the **area** *and* **perimeter** of each rectangle. Give them in simplified form.

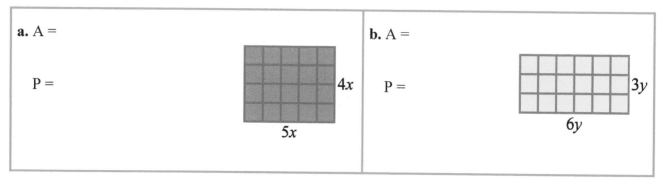

a. A =

   P =

$4x$

$5x$

b. A =

   P =

$3y$

$6y$

Skills Review 11

1. Solve using mental math.

a. 38 + _____ = 120	**b.** 460 + _____ = 1,000	**c.** 7 · 90 + _____ = 700

2. Write the statements as equations. Use a letter for the unknown.
   Then solve the equations.

   a. 36 less than a certain number gives us 487.

   Equation: _____   Solution: _____

   b. The product of 7 and a number is 105.

   Equation: _____   Solution: _____

   c. When you divide a number by 9, the result is 14.

   Equation: _____   Solution: _____

3. Round to the nearest...

Number	7,632,948,173	15,190,705,214	4,578,213,697	9,413,582,301
...ten million				
...hundred million				
...billion				

4. Richard drives at a constant speed of 45
   miles per hour.

   a. How far does he drive in 10 minutes?

   b. *Estimate* how many hours it would
   take him to drive 600 miles.

5. Simplify the expressions. Think of line segments to help you.

a. $x + x + x + x + 7$	**b.** $y + y + p + p + p + p$
c. $8s - s - s$	**d.** $40x - 9x + 5y$

Skills Review 12

1. Write an inequality for each phrase. You will need to choose a variable to represent the quantity in question.

   a. Spend no more than $12 on a new shirt.

   b. All participants must be at least 16 years old.

   c. There were fewer than 10 guests at the party.

2. Rewrite the expressions using an exponent, then solve them. You may use a calculator.

   a. $7 \cdot 7 \cdot 7 \cdot 7 \cdot 7 \cdot 7 \cdot 7 \cdot 7$

   b. $4 \cdot 4 \cdot 4 \cdot 4 \cdot 4 \cdot 4$

3. Write in expanded form, in two ways. Look at the model.

a. $7{,}325 = 7000 + 300 + 20 + 5$ $= 7 \times 10^3 + 3 \times 10^2 + 2 \times 10^1 + 5 \times 10^0$	**b.** 12,800
c. 2,400,703	

4. Write an expression for each situation, and simplify it.

   a. What is the area of a square with sides of length $12p$?

   b. What is the perimeter of a regular hexagon with sides of length $7x$?

5. Solve these equations. First, simplify what is on the left side.

a. $3y + 4y = 35$	**b.** $12x - 3x = 72$	**c.** $7a + 4a - 3a = 48$
$=$	$=$	$=$
$=$	$=$	$=$

6. Marilyn bought a used car for $4,380.
   She spent 3/4 of her savings on the car.
   How much were her savings originally?

Skills Review 13

1. Multiply using the distributive property.

a. $7(6 + a + b + 5) =$	**b.** $4(y + 9 + r) =$

2. Calculate the values of y according to the equation $y = 2x - 3$.

x	2	3	4	5	6	7
y	1					

Now, plot the points.

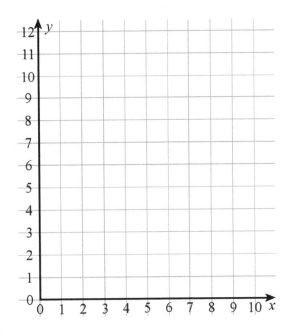

3. Allison and three of her friends shared equally the cost of renting a cabin for five days at $180 per day. How much did each one pay?

4. Eric's garden has a total area of 450 ft^2. He divided it into two sections: one for vegetables, and one for flowers. Eric's flower garden measures 15 ft by 6 ft. What is the area of his vegetable garden?

5. Divide. Below each division, check your result.

a. $73 \div 8 =$ _____ R _____

_____ · _____ + _____ = _____

b. $87 \div 12 =$ _____ R _____

_____ · _____ + _____ = _____

6. Solve using mental math.

a. $540 + 3 \cdot 13$

=

b. $16 + (720 - 450)$

=

19

Skills Review 14

1. Write as decimals.

   a. 9 and 17 thousandths   **b.** 58 hundredths

   c. 5 and 2641 millionths   **d.** 83 ten-thousandths

2. Find the value of the expressions if $p = 17$ and $s = 9$.

a. $40 - p - s$	**b.** $40 + (p - s)$

3. Kyle, Liam, and Justin shared the cost of buying a four-wheeler ATV that cost \$7,960 so that Kyle and Justin each paid twice as much as Liam. How much did each one pay?

4. Multiply.

a.	**b.**
$\begin{array}{r} 5\,9\,0\,2 \\ \times\ \ \ 8\,7\,3 \\ \hline \end{array}$	$\begin{array}{r} 7\,8\,1\,6 \\ \times\ \ \ 4\,0\,6 \\ \hline \end{array}$

5. Divide.

  a. $\dfrac{2{,}800}{40} =$ **b.** $\dfrac{630}{90} =$

  c. $\dfrac{16{,}000}{500} =$ **d.** $\dfrac{54{,}000}{60} =$

6. Fill in the table.

Expression	The terms in it	Coefficient(s)	Constants
$y \cdot 5$			
$7x^2y^6 + 12$			
$\dfrac{16}{29}y$			

Skills Review 15

1. Estimate the result using mental math and rounded numbers. Find the exact value using a calculator. Also, find the error of estimation. In **b.**, round your answer to one decimal digit.

a. $248{,}341 - 12 \cdot 3{,}127$ Estimation: Exact: Error of estimation:	**b.** $34{,}542 \div 731$ Estimation: Exact: Error of estimation:

2. **a.** Is $x = 7$ a root for the equation $x^2 - 19 = 29$?

   b. Find the root of the equation $a/6 = 12$ in the set $\{72, 86, 75, 81\}$.

3. Write in order from the smallest to the largest.

a. 0.12 0.00089 0.0024	**b.** 2.692 2.069 2.00999

4. Circle any numbers in each series of numbers that AREN'T factors of the underlined number.

   a. __348__   12   8   29   9   58

   b. __123__   16   7   38   23   4

   c. __580__   6   116   5   27   20

5. Each rectangular area model (not to scale) illustrates a multiplication. In each rectangular part, write how many square units its area is. Then, find the total area by adding the areas of the parts.

a. $34 \cdot 22$ 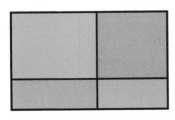	**b.** $49 \cdot 16$ 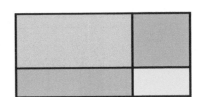

Skills Review 16

1. Calculate in columns. Remember to line up the decimal points.

   a. $9.0316 - 5.20178$

   b. $8 + 4.027 + 0.197036 + 7.9245$

2. Put parentheses into the equations to make them true.

   a. $8 \cdot 70 - 30 + 20 = 340$ **b.** $84 + 6 \div 6 - 15 = 0$ **c.** $260 - 80 + 50 \div 5 = 26$

3. Twenty-four neighbors shared the cost of buying a swing set that cost $7,410 and two park benches that cost $465 each. How much did each one pay?

4. Simplify the expressions by adding and subtracting like terms.

a. $7y + 9y + 3$	**b.** $12p^2 + 4p^2$
c. $10m - 4m + 3n + 5n$	**d.** $8y + 6x + 2 + 19y - 3x$

5. Use the clues to find sets of increasing *consecutive* numbers. All numbers are between 60 and 90.

   a. _____ < _____ < _____ < _____

        cube number   multiple of 13   multiple of 6   prime

   b. _____ < _____ < _____ < _____

        multiple of 26   prime   factor of 320   square number

6. Find the missing exponent.

a. $7^{\square} = 2{,}401$	**b.** $5^{\square} = 15{,}625$	**c.** $8^{\square} = 2{,}097{,}152$
$4^{\square} = 65{,}536$	$9^{\square} = 6{,}561$	$10^{\square} = 1{,}000{,}000{,}000$

Skills Review 17

1. Round the numbers to *one decimal digit*, and use the rounded numbers to *estimate* the answer.
   Then calculate the exact answer.

a. $3.73916 + 0.4652$ Estimate: Exact:	**b.** $7.695218 - 1.408361$ Estimate: Exact:

2. Solve using mental math.

a. $99 + $ _____ $= 382$	**b.** $463 + $ _____ $= 1{,}000$	**c.** $7 \cdot 80 + $ _____ $= 600$

3. Write an equation for each situation (even if you could easily solve the problem without an
   equation). Then solve the equation.

   a. Beth is 18 ½ years older than Seth. When Seth is 65, how old will Beth be?
   Hint: Choose a variable to represent what is asked (what is not known).

   b. The total cost of 32 vases is $272 . How much does one vase cost?

4. Think of the distributive property "backwards," and factor these sums. Think of divisibility!

a. $4x + 4 = $ ____ $(x + 1)$	**b.** $5y + 15 = 5($ ____ $+$ ____ $)$
c. $7x + 35 = $ ____ $($ ____ $+$ ____ $)$	**d.** $9x + 18y + 36 = $ ___$($ ____ $+$ ____ $+$ ____ $)$

Skills Review 18

1. Divide. For each division, write a corresponding multiplication sentence.

a.	b.	c.	d.
$0.54 \div 6 =$	$7.2 \div 8 =$	$0.009 \div 3 =$	$0.00096 \div 12 =$

2. The registration fee to attend a 3-day workshop was $1,475, and 64 people registered to attend. First, *estimate* how much they paid in total, and then find the exact amount.

Estimate:

Exact:

3. Write an expression, in simplified form, for both the area *and* perimeter of each compound shape.

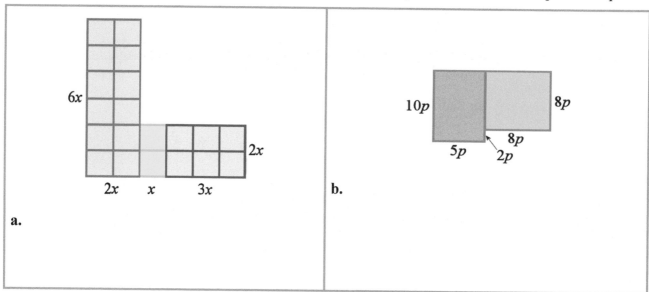

a.

b.

4. Write as pure fractions, *not* as mixed numbers—that is, the numerator (the number on the top) can be greater than the denominator (the number on the bottom).

   a. 0.00641   b. 0.009752   c. 3.0039

5. Plot these inequalities on the number line.

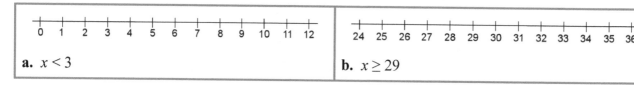

a. $x < 3$

b. $x \geq 29$

Skills Review 19

1. Multiply.

a. $0.8 \cdot 0.03 \cdot 0.5 =$	**b.** $0.7 \cdot 0.7 \cdot 0.7 =$
c. $4 \cdot 0.06 \cdot 0.009 =$	**d.** $8 \cdot 0.2 \cdot 0.0004 =$

2. Write an expression.

   a. the quantity $8x - 4$ divided by 6

   b. the quantity $9 + x$, cubed

   c. 7 times the quantity $x + 5$

   d. 2 times the sum of 3, x, and 7

3. For each graph, write the number pairs in the table. Then, write an equation that relates x and y.

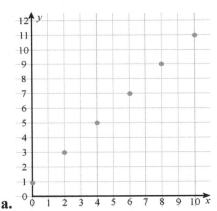

a.

x	0	2	4	6	8	10
y						

Equation: $y =$ _____

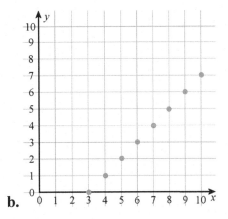

b.

x	3	4	5	6	7	8	9	10
y								

Equation: $y =$ _____

4. Cassandra had \$436.80 in savings. Then, she bought a microscope for \$142.99, a set of prepared microscope slides for \$27.73, and a microscope slide staining kit for \$37.95. How much money did she have left?

5. Solve. Notice carefully which operation(s) are done first.

a. $\dfrac{880}{8} + 3 \cdot 75 =$ _____	**b.** $120 \cdot 5 + \dfrac{3{,}600}{40} =$ _____

Skills Review 20

1. Divide. Round the answer to three decimals.

   a. $6\overline{)7.1\,0\,0\,0}$ **b.** $11\overline{)3}$ **c.** $3\overline{)8.5}$

2. Round to the nearest...

Number	3,975,491,872	9,184,702,537	19,963,261,583
...ten million			
...hundred million			
...billion			

3. Write any decimal number that can go in the space between the two numbers you are given. There are lots of possibilities!

a. 2.466 < _____ < 2.47	**b.** 7.26158 < _____ < 7.26941
c. 5.0281 < _____ < 5.1084	**d.** 3.629084 < _____ < 3.658173

4. Fill in the table.

numbers/letters	sum	difference	product	quotient
a. 24 and 6				
b. p and x				

Fill in the blanks so the equations are true.

Puzzle Corner

   a. $\dfrac{\boxed{} - \boxed{}}{10} = 48 - \dfrac{7}{10}$ **b.** $\dfrac{\boxed{} - 6}{7} = 4\dfrac{3}{7} - \dfrac{\boxed{}}{\boxed{}}$

Skills Review 21

1. Rewrite the expressions using an exponent, then solve them.

   a. 70 squared

   b. $5 \cdot 5 \cdot 5 \cdot 5 \cdot 5$

2. Add or subtract. First, change the fraction into a decimal.

a. $4\frac{7}{10} + 0.82$	**b.** $0.4 + \frac{57}{100}$	**c.** $5.49 + \frac{3}{10}$	**d.** $8\frac{953}{1000} - 0.4$

3. Find the value of these expressions.

a. $230 + 8 \cdot 10$	**b.** $7^2 \cdot 5^3$	**c.** $(620 - 140) \div 6 \cdot 10^4$

4. These are the ages of the members of a group of volunteer fire-fighters:

   28 20 25 24 19 23 32 18 26 30 27 29 31 22 34

   Find the average. Round your answer to the nearest whole number.

5. Frank drives a total of 28.6 km to work and back each day, five times a week. What distance does he drive in three weeks?

6. Simplify the expressions by adding and subtracting like terms.

a. $9x + 12x + 5$	**b.** $8z^7 + 14z^7$
c. $7m - 6m + 11n + 9n$	**d.** $6p + 8s + 4 + 13p - 5s$

7. Find a number that fits in place of the unknown.

a. $x \div 30 = 80$	**b.** $50 \cdot M = 7{,}000$	**c.** $900 - y = 440$

Skills Review 22

1. Write as decimals. Think of the equivalent fraction that has a denominator of 10, 100, or 1000.

a. $6\frac{24}{40}$	**b.** $\frac{35}{500}$	**c.** $4\frac{1}{4}$

2. Calculate without a calculator (using mental math and paper and pencil).

   a. $10^8 - 10^5 - 75{,}000$

   b. $6 \cdot 10^3 + 841{,}900 + 4 \cdot 10^7$

3. Find the missing number or variable in these area models.

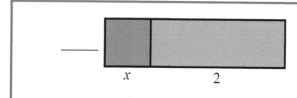
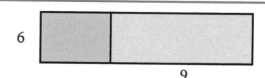

  a. ____ $(x + 2) = 4x + 8$ **b.** $6($ ____ $+ 9) = 6t + 54$

4. Round to...

Number:	0.470582	8.095326	1.5276301	0.853109	3.472635
...three decimals					
...five decimals					

5. **a.** Find the root of the equation $x^3 + 16 - 2x = 131$ in the set $\{1, 2, 3, 5, 7, 9\}$.

  b. Find the root of the equation $5x - 8 = 3x$ in the set $\{2, 3, 4, 5, 6\}$.

6. Evaluate the expressions when the value of the variable is given.

a. $4x + 39$ when $x = 6$	**b.** $\frac{72}{z} \cdot 15$ when $z = 9$

Skills Review 23

1. The Johnson family paid a total of $2,100 for groceries during the months of May and June. They paid $192 dollars more in June than in May. How much money did they spend on groceries in May?

   And in June?

2. Multiply or divide.

a.	b.	c.
$0.49 \div 100 =$	$1,000 \cdot 83.542 =$	$10^5 \cdot 42.73 =$
$2,600 \div 10,000 =$	$10^7 \cdot 0.003195 =$	$10^6 \cdot 8.03816 =$

3. Make up a situation from real life that could be described by the given inequality.

   a. $a < \$30$

   b. $g \geq 14$

   c. $p > 150$

4. Carol and five friends shared equally the cost of buying a badminton set that cost $246. How much did each one pay? (Use mental math.)

5. Find the missing side length when one side and the perimeter are given.

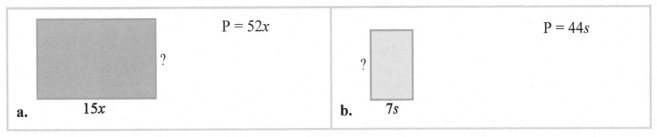

a. 15x   P = 52x

b. 7s   P = 44s

Skills Review 24

1. Multiply both the dividend and the divisor by the same number (10, 100, or 1000) so that you get a divisor that is a *whole number*. Then divide using long division.

a. $19.04 \div 0.8$	**b.** $8.236 \div 0.04$

2. First, simplify what is on the left side and what is on the right side. Then solve the equations.

a. $\quad 4x + 5x \ = \ 46 - 19$ $= $ $= $	**b.** $\quad 9c - c \ = \ 2 \cdot 60$ $= $ $= $	**c.** $\ 33x - 8x + 3x \ = \ 14 \cdot 60$ $= $ $= $

3. Write the decimals as fractions and multiply both.

a. $0.7 \ \cdot \ 0.05 \ = $ ↓ ↓ ↓	**b.** $0.006 \ \cdot \ 0.9 \ = $ ↓ ↓ ↓	**c.** $0.012 \ \cdot \ 0.0008 \ = $ ↓ ↓ ↓

4. Fill in the table.

expression	the terms in it	coefficient(s)	constants
$6s + 9y$			
$70p$			
$13x + 4$			

Skills Review 25

1. Which conversion is correct—the upper or the lower?

a. 7.38 ft = 7.38 · 12 in = 88.56 in	**b.** 30 qt = 30 · 4 gal = 120 gal
7.38 ft = $\dfrac{7.38}{12}$ in = 0.615 in	30 qt = $\dfrac{30}{4}$ gal = 7.5 gal

2. Estimate the result using mental math and rounded numbers. Find the exact value using a calculator. Also, find the error of estimation.

a. 153,270 − 46 · 2,267	**b.** 68,961 ÷ 543
Estimation:	Estimation:
Exact:	Exact:
Error of estimation:	Error of estimation:

3. Divide. Check your answer with multiplication. Round your answer to three decimals, if necessary.

a. $6\overline{)2.6\ 4}$ **b.** $22\overline{)4.8\ 8}$ **c.** $4\overline{)7}$

4. Ashley can type 40 words per minute. Consider the variables time (t), measured in minutes, and words (w).

a. Fill in the table.

b. Plot the points on the coordinate grid.

t (minutes)	0	1	2	3	4	5
w (words)						

c. Write an equation that relates t and w.

d. Which of the two variables is the independent variable?

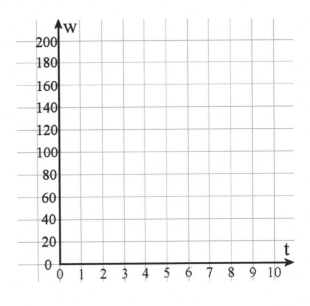

Skills Review 26

1. Divide using long division. Use a notebook. If the division is not even, give your answer to <u>two</u> decimal digits.

a. $197.59 \div 0.06$	**b.** $0.2 \div 0.0037$
c. $42 \div 0.008$	**d.** $91.43 \div 0.024$

2. A bag of peanut butter pretzels weighs 282 grams. A 30-gram serving contains 4.5 grams of fat. How many grams of fat does the whole bag of pretzels contain? (Round your answer to one decimal digit.)

3. Simplify the expressions and remove the unnecessary multiplication signs.

a. $y \cdot y \cdot y \cdot y$	**b.** $x \cdot x \cdot 8$
c. $7 \cdot p \cdot 2 \cdot 5$	**d.** $3 \cdot x \cdot y$

4. Write an expression. Then simplify or solve.

   a. First subtract 5.9 from 8.3, then multiply the result by 7.

   b. The quantity 4 times a, cubed.

   c. 5 times the quantity 9 minus 3, plus 9 times the quantity 8 plus 7.

5. Write these amounts using the basic units (meters, grams, or liters) by "translating" the prefixes. Use both fractions and decimals, like this: 6 cm = 6/100 m = 0.06 m (since "centi" means "hundredth part").

a. 6 cm = $6/100$ m = 0.06 m 8 mm = _____ m = _____ m	**b.** 4 cg = _____ g = _____ g 7 ml = _____ L = _____ L

Puzzle Corner   Find what is missing from the equations.

a. $378 + 2 \cdot 165 = 395 +$ ____ = _____   **b.** $735 \cdot 200 =$ ____ $\cdot 7{,}350 =$ _____

Skills Review 27

1. Factor these sums (writing them as products). Think of divisibility!

a. $18x + 12 =$ _____ (___ $x +$ ____)	**b.** $21x + 7z + 42 =$ ____ (____ $+$ ____ $+$ ____)

2. Convert between the units. Use a calculator when needed. Round your answers to two decimals.

1 in = 2.54 cm   1 foot = 0.3048 m
1 quart = 0.946 L   1 kg = 2.2 lb

a.	**b.**	**c.**	**d.**
65 cm = _____ in	9.4 m = _____ ft	7.8 L = _____ qt	0.927 kg = _____ lb

3. Solve using mental math.

a. $17 + (820 - 570)$	**b.** $94 + 48 + 26$	**c.** $420 \div 4 - 300 \div 6$
=	=	=

4. Kyle rides his bike 12 miles to work each day, at a constant speed of 16 miles an hour.

   a. What distance can Kyle ride his bike in 30 minutes?   In 15 minutes?

   b. What time does he need to leave home in order to arrive at work at 7:55 am?

5. Write as fractions and also as mixed numbers.

a. 4.0051	**b.** 20.69
c. 7.2069183	**d.** 140.317

6. Write an equation, and find the part that is not given.

Statement	Equation
a. The quotient is 9, the divisor is _____, the dividend is 108.	
b. The subtrahend is 67, the difference is 34, and the minuend is _____.	
c. The factors are 4, 9, and _____, and the product is 180.	

Skills Review 28

1. Find the missing factor or dividend.

a. 0.0009 · _____ = 9,000		
b. _____ · 0.28 = 2,800		
c. $\dfrac{21}{\rule{2cm}{0.4pt}}$ = 0.021	**d.** $\dfrac{6.9}{\rule{2cm}{0.4pt}}$ = 0.069	

2. Write in normal form (as a number).

a. $6 \cdot 10^3 + 9 \cdot 10^5 + 7 \cdot 10^0$

b. $8 \cdot 10^9 + 2 \cdot 10^6 + 5 \cdot 10^4 + 3 \cdot 10^1$

3. Write the ratios. Simplify to lowest terms.

   a. The ratio of roses to daisies

   b. The ratio of roses to all flowers

   c. The ratio of daisies to all flowers

4. Mark these decimals on the number line: 0.03   0.007   0.018   0.01   0.024   0.002   0.014

5. Cheryl has $89.40, Jared has 2/3 as much
   as Cheryl, and Louise has 1/4 as much
   as Jared. How much money do they have
   in total?

6. Melanie bought a 3-kg bag of brown sugar.
   She used 300 grams in a recipe, and then
   divided what was left equally into four bags.
   How much did each bag weigh?

7. Evaluate the expressions when the value of the variable is given.

a. $3x + 19$ when $x = 8$	**b.** $\dfrac{1}{4}s$ when $s = 1,200$

Skills Review 29

1. Write two different equations with a root $x = 14$.

2. Divide in parts, then add or subtract the results.

a. $\dfrac{200 - 40}{5}$	**b.** $\dfrac{480 + 32 - 8}{8}$	**c.** $\dfrac{18 \text{ ft } 9 \text{ in}}{6}$

3. Calculate in columns. Remember to line up the decimal points.

   a. $613 - 59.2 - 7.86923$

   b. $15 + 8.174 + 0.629438 + 3.4281$

4. Write an inequality that corresponds to the number line plot.

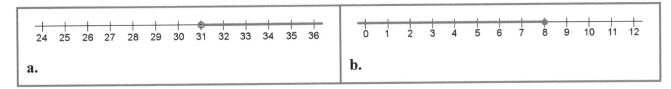

   a.   **b.**

5. Change to unit rates. Give the rate using the word "per" or the slash / .

   a. The airplane flew 3,850 miles in seven hours.

   b. Mrs. Jefferson used 36 yards of fabric to make 12 dresses.

6. Rewrite the expressions using an exponent, then solve them. You may use a calculator.

   a. $6 \cdot 6 \cdot 6 \cdot 6 \cdot 6$ **b.** $8 \cdot 8 \cdot 8 \cdot 8$

   c. 400 squared   **d.** 15 cubed

7. Convert to the given unit. Round your answers to two decimals, if needed.

a. 8 oz = _____ lb	**b.** 7.4 lb = _____ oz	**c.** 99 oz = _____ lb

Skills Review 30

1. Solve the equations.

a. $0.8x = 3.76$	**b.** $0.03x = 0.0096$

2. Carmen earns $96 in eight hours. How long will it take her to earn $144? Use the equivalent rates.

$$\frac{\$96}{8 \text{ hours}} = \frac{\$\boxed{}}{1 \text{ hour}} = \frac{\$144}{\boxed{} \text{ hours}}$$

3. Write an expression for each situation.

   a. 19 more than y

   b. the cost of a toy that originally cost x, but now is discounted by $8

4. Round the numbers to *one decimal digit*, and use the rounded numbers to *estimate* the answer. Then calculate the exact answer.

$7.5283 + 5 - 9.3024$

Estimate:

Exact:

Skills Review 31

1. Change into the basic unit (either meter, liter, or gram). Think of the meaning of the prefix.

    a. 5 cm =   **b.** 3 mg =   **c.** 16 ml =

2. An average adult can read 300 words per minute.

    a. Fill in the table.

    b. Plot the points on the coordinate grid.

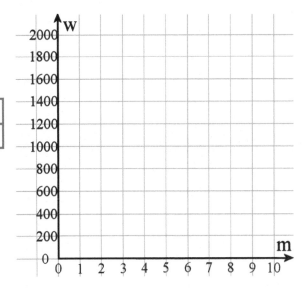

m (minutes)	0	1	2	3	4	5	6
w (words)	0	300					

    c. Write an equation that relates m and w.

    d. Which of the two variables is the independent variable?

3. A convenience store sells bottles of fruit juice in a ratio of 1:3:1:2 for the flavors apple, orange, grape, and pineapple, respectively.

    a. Draw a bar model. What is the ratio of bottles of pineapple juice to all the bottles of juice sold?

    b. For every 350 bottles of juice sold, how many of them are of each flavor?

4. Tag zeros on the dividend, so that the dividend and divisor have the same amount of decimal digits, and then divide mentally. Check by multiplication.

a. $0.9 \div 0.003 =$	**b.** $0.5 \div 0.01 =$	**c.** $0.04 \div 0.0002 =$

5. Round to the place of the underlined digit.

    a. 6<u>4</u>3,195 ≈ _____   **b.** 8,25<u>9</u>,813 ≈ _____

Skills Review 32

1. Which is more? (Write $<$, $=$, or $>$ between the measurements.) Use the "ballpark" figures in the chart.

a. 3 in 8 cm	**b.** 7 kg 12 lb		
c. 6 gal 18 L	**d.** 4 m 9 ft		

Ballpark figures:	1 m $\approx$ 1 yd 1 kg $\approx$ 2 lb
	1 L $\approx$ 1 qt 1 in $\approx$ 2.5 cm

2. Kay baked 96 cookies, some lemon and some chocolate. The ratio of lemon cookies to chocolate cookies was 1:3.

   a. Draw a bar model to represent the situation.

   b. How many lemon cookies did she bake?

   c. How many chocolate cookies did she bake?

3. Find the value of these expressions.

a. $(5+5)^4 \cdot (13-4)^2$	**b.** $90 + 50 \div 5 \cdot 7 - 3$	**c.** $\dfrac{6^2}{6} \cdot 6$

4. Find the unit prices for the following items. Round to the nearest cent. Use a notebook for calculations.

Item and price	Unit price	What would this cost...?	
36 oz of cereal for $5.98		8 oz of cereal	
20 lb of rice for $18.52		3.5 lb of rice	
4 lb of beans for $5.22		1.9 lb of beans	

5. Simplify the expressions.

a. $8a + 6 + 2a - 9x$	**b.** $y + y + z + 7 + x$

6. Find a number that fits in place of the unknown.

a. $5{,}600 \div x = 80$	**b.** $40 \cdot M = 36{,}000$	**c.** $z - 900 = 640$

Skills Review 33

1. Multiply using the distributive property.

a. $12(8c + 6a) =$
b. $7(2 + 5a + 9b) =$
c. $p(x + 9) =$

2. Write as decimals.

a. $80 + 5 + \dfrac{4}{100} + \dfrac{9}{1000} + \dfrac{6}{10}$
b. $200 + \dfrac{3}{1000} + \dfrac{7}{100,000} + \dfrac{5}{100}$

3. A rectangle's width is four times its height, and its perimeter is 150 cm. Find the rectangle's width and its height.

4. Divide. Add a decimal point and decimal zeros to the dividend. If the division does not come out exactly, then round the answer to three decimals.

a. $7\overline{)3}$

b. $12\overline{)47}$

c. $8\overline{)91}$

Place the digits from the orange box in the empty boxes so that the total of each row and column matches the description in parentheses.

43	19	15
20	36	21

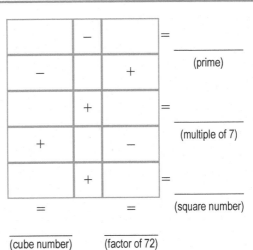

Skills Review 34

1. Use the given ratios to convert the measuring units. Round your answers to one decimal digit.

a. Use $1 = \dfrac{2.54 \text{ cm}}{1 \text{ in}}$ to convert 83 inches to centimeters.	
83 in =	
b. Use $1 = \dfrac{1 \text{ mi}}{1.6093 \text{ km}}$ to convert 78 km to miles.	
78 km =	

2. The area of a square is $16x^2$. What is the length of each side?

3. Multiply.

a. $0.04 \cdot 0.0007 =$	**b.** $0.002 \cdot 0.9 =$	**c.** $0.05 \cdot 0.3 =$

4. One set of luggage used to cost \$169.95 but is now discounted by 1/5 of its price.
   Another set of luggage used to cost \$145.60 but is now discounted by 1/8 of its price.

   The Williams family bought one set of the more expensive luggage and two sets of the cheaper luggage. How much money did they spend in total?

5. In these problems, you see both fractions and decimals. Either change the decimal into a fraction, or vice versa. You decide which way is easier! Then, calculate mentally.

a. $0.7 + \dfrac{1}{4}$	**b.** $0.63 + 4\dfrac{4}{10}$	**c.** $3\dfrac{2}{5} + 8.9$	**d.** $\dfrac{6}{100} - 0.05$

Skills Review 35

1. Find the missing factor or divisor.

a. $0.0032 \cdot$ _____ $= 320$	**b.** _____ $\cdot \, 0.00714 = 0.714$
c. $\dfrac{26}{} = 0.026$ **d.** $\dfrac{5.1}{} = 0.051$	**e.** $\dfrac{803}{} = 8.03$ **f.** $\dfrac{0.49}{} = 0.049$

2. **a.** Draw a picture in which (1) there are four triangles for each six circles, and (2) there is a total of 12 circles.

   b. Write the ratio of all triangles to all circles, and simplify this ratio to lowest terms.

   c. Write the ratio of all shapes to triangles, and simplify this to lowest terms.

3. Write as percentages, fractions, and decimals.

a. $72\% = \dfrac{}{} =$ _____	**b.** _____ $= \dfrac{4}{100} =$ _____	**c.** _____ $\% = \dfrac{}{} = 0.26$

4. Compare and write $<$, $>$, or $=$.

   a. $10^5 - 1000 \;\square\; 10^4$ **b.** $10^6 + 10^3 \;\square\;$ one billion   **c.** $7 \times 10^8 \;\square\; 6 \times 10^9$

5. Fill in the table.

numbers/letters	sum	difference	product	quotient
a. 27 and 3				
b. p and y				

6. **a.** Solve the inequality $x - 9 > 12$ in the set $\{8, 14, 17, 22, 31\}$.

   b. Solve the inequality $x + 6 \leq 15$ in the set $\{2, 5, 9, 14, 17\}$.

7. Add.

a. $0.7 + 0.03 =$	**b.** $0.02 + 0.00005 =$	**c.** $0.00008 + 0.006 =$

Skills Review 36

1. Find the value of the expressions.

a. $10^3 - 7 \cdot 80$	**b.** $\dfrac{1}{6} \cdot 42 - 5$	**c.** $\dfrac{200 \cdot 60}{30 \cdot 10}$

2. **a.** If Laura walks 420 meters in five minutes,
   What is the unit rate at which Laura is walking?

   b. How many minutes will it take her to walk 756 meters,
   if she keeps walking at the same rate?

3. Solve these equations. First, simplify what is on the left side and what is on the right side.
   Then solve.

a. $\quad 5x + 2x \;=\; 62 - 13$	**b.** $\quad 8c - c \;=\; 3 \cdot 70$	**c.** $\quad 12x - 7x + 3x \;=\; 6 \cdot 80$
$=$	$=$	$=$
$=$	$=$	$=$

4. One hundred forty-six people attended the Hill
   Family Reunion. Of those who attended, 86
   were age 40 or older, and the rest were younger.
   Find what percentage of the people were age 40
   or older, and what percentage were younger.

5. Write in order from the smallest to the largest.

a. 0.417 0.9 0.0864	**b.** 2.68 2.836 2.638

6. Convert to the given unit. Round your answers to two decimals, if needed.

a. 7.2 gal = _____ qt	**c.** 91 fl. oz. = _____ qt	**e.** 0.073 T = _____ lb
b. 8.5 qt = _____ fl. oz.	**d.** 638 qt = _____ gal	**f.** 5,600 lb = _____ T

Skills Review 37

1. Write the equivalent rates.

a. $\dfrac{525 \text{ mi}}{7 \text{ hr}} = \dfrac{}{1 \text{ hr}} = \dfrac{}{20 \text{ min}} = \dfrac{}{40 \text{ min}}$	**b.** $\dfrac{\$18}{45 \text{ min}} = \dfrac{}{15 \text{ min}} = \dfrac{}{1 \text{ hr}} = \dfrac{}{1 \text{ hr } 45 \text{ min}}$

2. Find the percentages. Use mental math.

a. 10% of 50 kg _____	**b.** 10% of $32 _____	**c.** 10% of 15 mi _____
30% of 50 kg _____	40% of $32 _____	60% of 15 mi _____

3. Write the decimals as fractions and multiply both.

a. $0.8 \cdot 0.07 =$ ↓ ↓ ↓	**b.** $0.006 \cdot 0.2 =$ ↓ ↓ ↓	**c.** $0.015 \cdot 0.0003 =$ ↓ ↓ ↓

4. Express the volume (V) or area (A) as a multiplication, and solve.

a. A cube with edges each 4 inches long: V = _____	**b.** A square with a side length of 9 cm: A = _____

5. Write an expression for the perimeter as a multiplication, and then simplify it.

a. ____ (____ + ____) = 	**b.** ____ (____ + ____) = 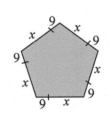

6. Divide using long division. Use a notebook. If the division is not even, give your answer to <u>two</u> decimal digits.

a. $273.19 \div 0.8 =$	**b.** $8.4165 \div 0.0037 =$

Skills Review 38

1. The rectangular area model illustrates the multiplication 68 · 45. In each rectangular part, write how many square units its area is. Then, find the total area by adding the areas of the parts.

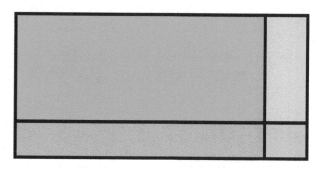

2. Estimate the result using mental math and rounded numbers. Find the exact value using a calculator. Also, find the error of estimation.

$148,516 - 12 \cdot 1,746$

Estimation:

Exact:

Error of estimation:

3. A certain brand of pencil costs 15 cents each. How many can you buy with $3.25? (Use mental math.)

4. Farmer Davis owns turkeys, ducks, and chickens in a ratio of 2:5:7. If he has 45 ducks, find (a) how many turkeys he has, and (b) how many chickens he has.

5. Use a calculator to find percentages of these quantities.

   a. 38% of $7,600   **b.** 84% of 52 m   **c.** 26% of 9.3 kg

6. Write the measurements in the place value charts.

  a. 19.8 hm 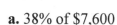   **b.** 32 cl

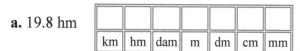   

  c. Use the chart to do these conversions:

    19.8 hm = _____ dam = _____ m = _____ dm

    32 cl = _____ dl = _____ l = _____ dal

Skills Review 39

1. All these items are on sale. Find the discounted price.

a. Price: $52
    10% off
 	
 Discount amount: $_____
 	
 Discounted price: $_____
	b. Price: $35
	    30% off
	
	 Discount amount: $_____
	
	 Discounted price: $_____
		c. Price: $160 
		    20% off
		
		 Discount amount: $_____
		
		 Discounted price: $_____

2. A flower bed is four times as long as it is wide.

   a. What is its aspect ratio?

   b. The perimeter of the flower bed is 30 ft.
      Find its length and width.

   c. Find its area.

3. Simplify the expressions and remove the unnecessary multiplication signs.

a. $x \cdot x \cdot 8 \cdot 12 \cdot x \cdot x \cdot x$	**b.** $p \cdot 9 \cdot 5 - 6 \cdot 3$

4. Martin jogs at a constant speed of six miles per hour. Consider the variables time (t), measured in hours, and distance jogged (d), measured in miles.

   a. Fill in the table.

   b. Plot the points on the coordinate grid.

t (hours)	1	3	5	7	9	11	13
d (miles)	6	18					

   c. Write an equation that relates t and d.

   d. Which of the two variables is the independent variable?

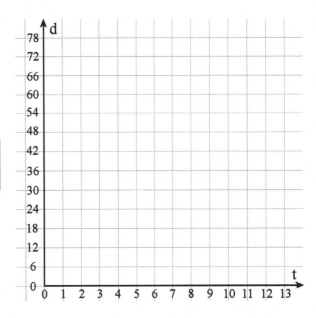

5. These are the ages of the members of an art club for kids:
   12 16 13 9 14 13 8 10 11 9 15 16 12 10 14 13 11 16 14 12
   Find the average, and round your answer to the nearest whole number.

Skills Review 40

1. Divide using long division. Round the answers to three decimal digits.

a. $928.46 \div 8$	**b.** $55.271 \div 13$

2. Alex and Carl picked strawberries in a ratio of 3:5. If Carl has 26 more strawberries than Alex, how many strawberries does Alex have?

3. Use mental math to find the percentages.

a. Mia washed 10 of her 25 shirts. Mia washed _____% of her shirts.	**b.** Only 8 of 40 people at a party drank coffee. Only _____% of the people drank coffee.

4. Write an expression. Solve.

   a. 7 times the quantity 12 minus 9, plus 5 times the quantity 11 plus 8.

   b. The difference of 132 and 24, divided by the quantity 3 cubed.

5. Think of the distributive property "backwards," and factor these sums. Think of divisibility!

a. $9x + 54 = $ _____ (_____ + _____)	**b.** $6x - 24y + 36 = $ _____ (_____ − _____ + _____)

6. Write in expanded form, as a sum. Follow the example.

   a. $8.46 = 8 \cdot 1 + 4 \cdot \dfrac{1}{10} + 6 \cdot \dfrac{1}{100}$

   b. 0.739

   c. 52.1

7. Convert between the units. Use a calculator when needed. Round your answers to two decimals.
   Use the following conversion factors: 1 in = 2.54 cm; 1 ft = 0.3048 m; 1 qt = 0.946 L; 1 kg = 2.2 lb.

a.	**b.**	**c.**	**d.**
7 cm = _____ in	8.3 m = _____ ft	5 L = _____ qt	0.741 kg = _____ lb

Skills Review 41

1. Round to...

Number:	0.582631	9.317468
...three decimals		
...four decimals		
...five decimals		

2. Write as fractions and also as mixed numbers.

a. 5.0262

b. 8.1479306

3. Write an expression, in simplified form, for both the area *and* perimeter of the shape.

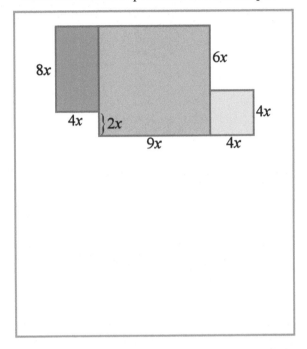

4. Last Friday, 20% of the customers at Mary's Restaurant ate chicken. If 13 customers ate chicken, how many customers ate there that day?

5. A microscope was discounted by 1/8 of its price, and now costs $168. Another microscope was discounted by 1/6 of its price and now costs $115. Find how much the two microscopes cost in total <u>before</u> the discount.

6. Use the given ratios to convert the measuring units. Round your answers to one decimal digit.

a. Use $1 = \dfrac{28.35 \text{ g}}{1 \text{ oz}}$ to convert 129 oz to grams.

129 oz =

b. Use $1 = \dfrac{1 \text{ mi}}{1.6093 \text{ km}}$ to convert 35 miles to km.

35 mi =

Skills Review 42

1. Find the prime factorization of these composite numbers.

a. 248	b. 165	c. 312

2. Write in order from the smallest to the largest.

a. 0.073 0.37 0.09	b. 5.280 5.208 5.028

3. Write an expression.

   a. 8 added to the product $5s$ **b.** The difference of $6y$ and 7

   c. w^4 divided by the quantity $w - 2$ **d.** The quantity 9 minus m, squared

4. Multiply or divide.

a.	b.	c.
$2,900 \div 10,000 =$	$100 \cdot 86.127 =$	$10^1 \cdot 0.03062 =$

5. Write ratios of the given quantities. Use the fraction line to write the ratios. Then, simplify the ratios. In each problem, you will need to *convert* one quantity so it has the same measuring unit as the other.

a. 4 lb and 12 oz	b. 7 m and 21 cm

6. Write the fractions with a denominator of 100, and then write them as percentages.

a. $\dfrac{6}{10} = \dfrac{\ \ \ \ }{100} = $ _____ %	b. $\dfrac{9}{20} = \dfrac{\ \ \ \ }{100} = $ _____ %	c. $\dfrac{8}{25} = \dfrac{\ \ \ \ }{100} = $ _____ %

Skills Review 43

1. Convert to the given unit. Round your answers to two decimals, if needed.

a. 8 in = _____ ft	**b.** 17.3 ft = _____ in	**c.** 5 3/4 ft = _____ in

2. Calculate in columns.

   a. $6 + 5.301 + 0.729068 + 3.2815$

   b. $633 - 75.4 - 8.71924$

3. **a.** Solve the inequality $4x - 13 \geq 35$ in the set {9, 10, 11, 12, 13, 14}.

   b. Solve the inequality $9 < y + 3$ in the set {4, 5, 6, 7, 8, 9}.

4. Gayle made a large quilt that contained 400 squares. Of them, 60 were purple, 132 were yellow, and the rest were blue. Find what percentage of the squares were purple, what percentage were yellow, and what percentage were blue.

5. Change to unit rates. Give the rate using the word "per" or the slash / .

   a. Eric drove 440 miles in eight hours.

   b. There are 620 calories in four ounces of chocolate.

6. Simplify the fractions. Divisibility tests will help.

a. $\dfrac{36}{72}$	**b.** $\dfrac{40}{96}$	**c.** $\dfrac{26}{65}$

Skills Review 44

1. **a.** Six scented candles cost $24. Fill in the table of rates. The variable P stands for price, and c for candles.

P						24				
c	1	2	3	4	5	6	7	8	9	10

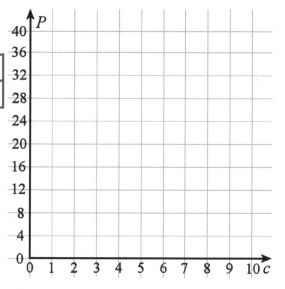

   b. Each number pair in the table *is* a rate, but we can also view them as <u>points</u> with two coordinates. Plot the number pairs in the coordinate grid.

   c. Write an equation relating the price (P) and the number of candles (c).

2. Find the greatest common factor of the numbers.

a. 140 and 76
b. 90 and 132

3. Multiply.

a. $2.5 \cdot 0.04 \cdot 0.6 =$
b. $9 \cdot 0.07 \cdot 0.003 =$
c. $3 \cdot 0.5 \cdot 0.08 =$
d. $4 \cdot 0.009 \cdot 0.2 =$

4. Jay had $560 in savings. Then he spent 20% of it on a digital camera. How much did the camera cost? (Use mental math.)

5. Write an equivalent division problem where the divisor is a whole number. Then solve with long division.

a. $\dfrac{64.82}{0.07}$	**b.** $\dfrac{55.26}{0.009}$

Skills Review 45

1. Write the multiplications as expressions of a "percentage of the number".

a. 0.04 · 9	**b.** 0.22 · $700	**c.** 0.8 · 30 kg
____% of _____ = _____	____% of _____ = _____	____% of _____ = _____

2. Mr. Thompson's orchard has lemon, orange, and grapefruit trees in a ratio of 2:7:5.
   If there are 12 lemon trees, find (a) how many trees the orchard has in total,
   (b) how many are orange trees, and (c) how many are grapefruit trees.

3. First find the GCF of the numbers. Then factor the expressions using the GCF.

a. GCF of 18 and 30 is _____   18 + 30 = ____ · ____ + ____ · ____ = ____ (____ + ____)
b. GCF of 72 and 48 is _____   72 + 48 = ____ (____ + ____)

4. Fill in the table.

Expression	The terms in it	Coefficient(s)	Constants
$3p^2y^5 - 17$			
$\dfrac{9}{14}x$			

5. Change into the basic unit (either meter, liter, or gram). Think of the meaning of the prefix.

   a. 74 km =   **b.** 15 ml =   **c.** 283 mg =

6. Divide. For each division, write a corresponding multiplication sentence.

a. 0.54 ÷ 0.09 =	**b.** 4.8 ÷ 0.8 =	**c.** 0.096 ÷ 0.012 =

Skills Review 46

1. Write as fractions, *not* as mixed numbers (the numerator can be greater than the denominator).

   a. 3.7052   **b.** 8.421825   **c.** 5.9430176

2. **a.** The perimeter of a square is 48 m. What is its area?

   b. The volume of a cube is 216 cubic inches. How long is its (one) edge?

3. Find the value of these expressions.

a. $59 + 72 \div 6 \cdot 8 - 37$	**b.** $\dfrac{9^2}{3^3}$	**c.** $10^4 \cdot (60 + 80) \div 7$

4. Melissa bought three meters of ribbon, and cut it into sections that were 0.4 meters long.

   a. How many sections did she get?

   b. How much ribbon did she have left?

5. Find the percentage of discount.

   a. A drone: original price, $160; discounted price, $112.

   b. A 3-D puzzle: original price, $104; discounted price, $78.

6. Shelly's house is three times as long as it is wide.

   a. What is its aspect ratio?

   b. The perimeter of her house is 144 ft.
   Find its length and width.

   c. Find its area.

7. Find the LCM of these numbers.

a. 6 and 8	**b.** 4 and 9

Skills Review 47

1. Add or subtract the fractions.

a. $\dfrac{2}{9} + \dfrac{1}{6} + \dfrac{2}{5}$	**b.** $\dfrac{11}{12} - \dfrac{1}{8} - \dfrac{1}{3}$

2. Dana and Mitch bought a surfboard for $249 and shared the cost so that Mitch paid $55 more than Dana. How much did each one pay?

3. Find the prime factorization of these composite numbers.

a. 117	**b.** 215	**c.** 370

4. Divide. If the division does not come out exactly, then round the answer to three decimals.

a. $12\overline{)9}$ **b.** $5\overline{)6\,3}$ **c.** $7\overline{)3\,2.4}$

Skills Review 48

1. Convert between the units. Use a calculator when needed. Round your answers to two decimals.

a.	**b.**	**c.**	Conversion Factors:
2 cm = _____ in	3 m = _____ yd	1 L = _____ qt	1 inch = 2.54 cm
14.2 in = _____ cm	8.7 m = _____ ft	6.4 qt = _____ L	1 foot = 0.3048 m
			1 quart = 0.946 L

2. Add or subtract. Give your answer as a mixed number when possible, and in lowest terms.

a. $8\frac{1}{6} - 5\frac{1}{15}$	**b.** $\frac{9}{10} + \frac{4}{100}$	**c.** $11\frac{6}{7} - 7\frac{13}{20}$

3. Multiply using the distributive property.

a. $4(8 + 12s) =$	**b.** $9(5x + 7 + 3y) =$

4. Write as decimals.

a. $\dfrac{915}{10,000}$
b. $2\dfrac{4013}{100,000}$
c. $\dfrac{6238}{1,000,000}$

5. Round to...

Number:	0.753824	2.6402769
...one decimal		
...four decimals		
...five decimals		

6. Simplify the fractions to lowest terms, or simplify before you multiply the fractions.

a. $\dfrac{54}{96}$	**b.** $\dfrac{5}{12} \cdot \dfrac{3}{5} =$	**c.** $\dfrac{27}{63}$

Skills Review 49

1. Find the greatest common factor of the given numbers.

a. 48, 96, and 132	b. 64, 88, and 120

2. Multiply. Give your answers as mixed numbers. Put the fractional part into lowest terms.

a. $\dfrac{3}{8} \cdot 4\dfrac{1}{6}$	b. $3\dfrac{4}{5} \cdot 5 \cdot \dfrac{1}{3}$

3. Use ratios to convert the measuring units. Round your answers to one decimal digit.

	Conversion factors:
a. 59 cm into inches	1 in = 2.54 cm
	1 kg = 2.2 lb
b. 27 kg into pounds	

4. Simplify the expressions and remove the unnecessary multiplication signs.

a. $x \cdot x \cdot 5 \cdot 8 - 4 \cdot 3$	b. $y \cdot 7 + 9$

5. Divide mentally in parts. First, think how the dividend can be written in two or more parts.
   One of the parts will not be evenly divisible by the divisor.

a. $\dfrac{601}{6} = \dfrac{600+1}{6} = 100\dfrac{1}{6}$	b. $\dfrac{607}{3}$	c. $\dfrac{8,021}{4}$	d. $\dfrac{517}{5}$

6. Write as percentages, fractions, and decimals.

a. $80\% = \dfrac{}{} = \underline{}$	b. $\underline{}\% = \dfrac{15}{100} = \underline{}$	c. $\underline{}\% = \dfrac{}{} = 0.04$

Skills Review 50

1. Kevin took the results from a survey that his parents did at their restaurant and made a frequency table. Then, he drew a bar graph.

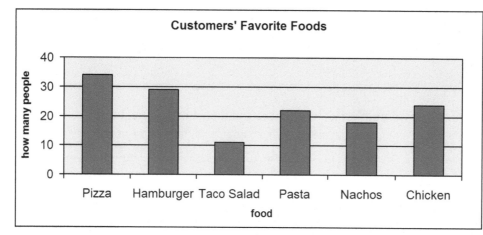

Customers' Favorite Foods

Favorite Food	Frequency
Pizza	34
Hamburger	29
Taco Salad	11
Pasta	22
Nachos	18
Chicken	24
TOTAL	138

a. Let's say that the restaurant has about 700 customers each week. Based on the survey results, estimate about how many people might order nachos next week.

b. Do the same for hamburger.

2. Look at the picture of the puppies and kittens. If we drew more puppies and kittens in the same ratio, how many puppies would there be…

a. … for 12 kittens?

b. … for 60 kittens?

3. A pair of wireless headphones costs four times as much as a pair of sports headphones. Buying one pair of each would cost $98.75. How much would it cost to buy three pairs of sports headphones?

4. First find the GCF of the numbers. Then factor the expressions using the GCF.

a. GCF of 84 and 60 is _____   84 + 60 = ____ (____ + ____)
b. GCF of 49 and 63 is _____   49 + 63 = ____ (____ + ____)

5. Simplify before you multiply.

a. $\dfrac{4}{6} \cdot \dfrac{6}{8}$
b. $\dfrac{9}{15} \cdot \dfrac{8}{10}$

Skills Review 51

1. Find the missing side length when one side and the perimeter are given.

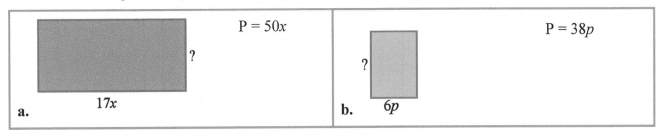

2. Find the reciprocal numbers. Then write a multiplication with the given number and its reciprocal.

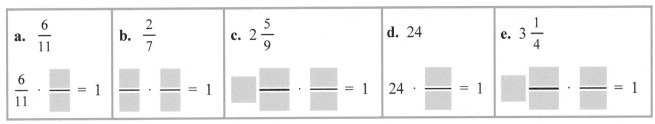

3. Marlene used 30% of her pay check to buy vases and now she has $595 left. How much money did she get in her pay check?

4. Find the least common multiple of the numbers.

a. 25 and 20	**b.** 40 and 50

5. **a.** Mr. Crawford's harvesting crew can pick 120 bushels of grapefruit in 8 hours. What is the unit rate at which they pick bushels of grapefruit?

   b. How many bushels could they pick in 14 hours?

6. Compare the numbers and write $<$, $=$, or $>$.

   a. 0.0001 ☐ 0.0000098   **b.** 34 millionths ☐ 0.000034   **c.** 67 hundredths ☐ 89 millionths

7. Convert the measurements. You can write the numbers in the place value chart or count the steps.

   a. 78 kl = _____ cl   **c.** 0.493 hl = _____ L

   b. 13.5 dl = _____ kl   **d.** 652 ml = _____ dal

	kl	hl	dal	L	dl	cl	ml

Skills Review 52

1. Multiply both the dividend and the divisor by some number so that you get a divisor that is a *whole number*. Then divide using long division.

a. $36.8 \div 0.4$	**b.** $0.7092 \div 0.09$

2. Solve.

a. There are 1 8/12 pies left over and four people share them equally. How much does each person get?	**b.** There are 1 1/3 burritos left over and two people share them equally. How much does each person get?

3. Ken drove 440 miles in eight hours, and Ed drove 325 miles in five hours. Which one drove faster?

4. *Estimate* the discounted price.

   a. 40% off of a $60.95 lamp

   b. 18% off of a $19.50 blouse

5. Round to the place of the underlined digit.

   a. $36\underline{5},499 \approx$ _____

   b. $6\underline{3}5,802,314 \approx$ _____

6. Write an equation, and find the part that is not given.

Statement	Equation
a. The factors are 9, 5, and 7, and the product is _____.	
b. The addends are 24, 89, and _____, and the sum is 200.	

Skills Review 53

1. Write as decimals.

a. $40 + 8 + \dfrac{2}{1000} + \dfrac{9}{100} + \dfrac{4}{10}$	**b.** $5 + \dfrac{7}{100} + \dfrac{3}{1000} + \dfrac{5}{1,000,000}$

2. Pickles the Chihuahua is 9 inches tall and weighs 8 pounds. Mustard the Labrador Retriever is 25 inches tall and weighs 80 pounds.

   a. How many percent is the smaller dog's height of the bigger dog's height?

   b. How many percent is the smaller dog's weight of the bigger dog's weight?

3. Find the value of the expressions if $x = 17$ and $y = 9$.

a. $5y + x$	**b.** $60 - (x + y)$

4. Students at a foreign language institute studied Spanish, French, German, and Chinese in a ratio of 5:3:2:1, respectively. If 16 students studied German, find out how many students studied each of the other three languages.

5. The unknown is given as a part of a part. Solve for x.

1/8	x		
1/4 of all	1/4 of all	1/4 of all	1/4 of all

$\vdash$———————— 576 ————————$\dashv$

6. Convert to the given unit. Round your answers to two decimals, if needed.
   (Remember, 1 mile = 5,280 ft)

   a. 5.3 mi = _____ ft   **b.** 6,100 yd = _____ mi   **c.** 9.24 mi = _____ yd

Skills Review 54

1. Fill in the blanks.

a. 3/5 of a number is 45.	**b.** 5/8 of a number is 60.	**c.** If 4/11 of a number is 48, what is the number?
1/5 of that number is _____.	1/8 of that number is _____.	
The number is _____.	The number is _____.	

2. Eva painted a painting on a canvas whose dimensions (the two sides) were 20″ by 30″.

   a. Write the aspect ratio, and simplify it to lowest terms.

   b. Eva also painted a smaller painting whose dimensions were 2/5 of the dimensions of the larger painting. What were its dimensions?

3. Find the percentages. Use mental math.

a. 20% of 70 kg _____	**b.** 60% of 40 kg _____	**c.** 1% of $50 _____

4. Convert between the units. Round your answers to two decimals.

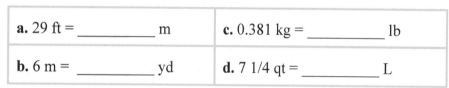

a. 29 ft = _____ m	**c.** 0.381 kg = _____ lb
b. 6 m = _____ yd	**d.** 7 1/4 qt = _____ L

Conversion Factors:
1 yard = 0.9144 m
1 lb = 0.454 kg
1 quart = 0.946 L

5. Make up a situation from real life that could be described by the given inequality.

   a. $a < 15$

   b. $g \geq 9$

   c. $p > 375$

6. Solve the equations.

a. $0.0072 + x = 1.9$	**b.** $x - 0.58307 = 1.30214$	**c.** $x + 2.70914 = 3.0092$

Skills Review 55

1. Put parentheses into the equations to make them true.

   a. $300 - 50 \cdot 40 + 20 = 15,000$ **b.** $400 \div 60 - 10 \cdot 12 = 96$ **c.** $70 + 80 \cdot 2 - 60 = 240$

2. Write an integer appropriate to each situation.

   a. Karen owes $67.

   b. Rodney climbed the 6,759 meter tall mountain.

   c. The temperature is 6°C below zero.

3. Multiply or divide. Use mental math.

a. $0.072 \div 0.006$	**b.** $5 \cdot 0.9 =$	**c.** $0.84 \div 12$

4. Use a calculator to find percentages of these quantities.

   a. 19% of $3700   **b.** 8% of 38 m   **c.** 67% of 8.5 kg

5. Which of the numbers 0, 1, 2 or 3 make the equation $\dfrac{y+8}{y+2} = 3$ true?

6. Earl and Matthew shared the cost of buying a riding lawn mower in a ratio of 3:5. Matthew paid $550 more than Earl. How much did the mower cost?

7. Find the prime factorization of these composite numbers.

a. 249	**b.** 150	**c.** 528

Skills Review 56

1. Solve the equations.

a. $\dfrac{h}{0.6} = 0.04$	**b.** $7z = 0.049$	**c.** $0.5d = 0.35$

2. Simplify the fractions to lowest terms, or simplify before you multiply the fractions.

a. $\dfrac{54}{72}$	**b.** $\dfrac{40}{180}$	**c.** $\dfrac{5}{8} \cdot \dfrac{24}{30} =$

3. Multiply using the distributive property.

a. $8(5a + 3) =$	**b.** $6(7x + 2y) =$	**c.** $5(4x + 9 + 8y) =$

4. Find the percentage of discount.

    a. An aquarium tank: original price, $75; discounted price, $60.

    b. A ham radio: original price, $156; discounted price, $117.

5. Convert the fractions into equivalent fractions with a denominator of 100, and then write them as percentages.

a. $\dfrac{7}{10} = \dfrac{}{100} = \underline{}\%$	**b.** $\dfrac{15}{25} = \dfrac{}{100} = \underline{}\%$	**c.** $\dfrac{19}{20} = \dfrac{}{100} = \underline{}\%$

6. Find the distances between the points.

    a. $(15, 42)$ and $(15, -27)$

    b. $(-53, 17)$ and $(-34, 17)$

7. Round the decimals to the underlined place.

    a. $0.4275\underline{5}92$

    b. $3.7\underline{4}208$

    c. $0.61\underline{9}5137$

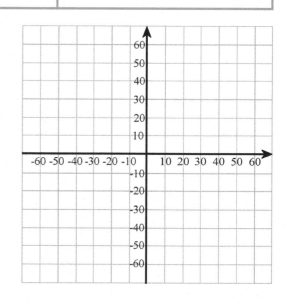

Skills Review 57

1. Add or subtract. You can think of number line jumps.

a. $6 - 8 =$
b. $^-4 - 2 =$
c. $^-9 + 6 =$
d. $^-2 + 5 =$

2. Find the greatest common factor of the numbers.

a. 84 and 147
b. 75 and 135

3. Of the 70 guests at a party, 30% of them drank coffee, and the rest drank punch. How many guests drank punch?

4. Find the missing exponent.

a. $6^{\square} = 7{,}776$	**b.** $11^{\square} = 14{,}641$	**c.** $9^{\square} = 531{,}441$

5. Use ratios to convert the measuring units. Round your answers to one decimal digit.
(Remember, 1 ft = 0.3048 m and 1 qt = 0.946 L)

a. 93 ft into meters
b. 47 liters into quarts

6. Carl kept track of how many points he got every time he played a certain game:

53 47 61 49 41 50 36 65 54 39 68 43 51 61 38

Find the average, and round to the nearest whole number.

7. Add or subtract the fractions.

a. $\dfrac{2}{9} + \dfrac{6}{7} + \dfrac{4}{21}$	**b.** $\dfrac{14}{15} - \dfrac{2}{3} - \dfrac{1}{10}$

Skills Review 58

1. Write the number pairs in the table. Then, write an equation that relates x and y.

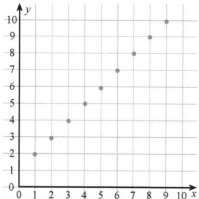

x	1	2	3	4	5	6	7	8	9
y									

Equation: $y =$ _____

2. Write the equivalent ratios. Think about equivalent fractions.

a. $3 : 5 = 15 :$ _____	**b.** $4 : 7 = 16 :$ _____

3. Write these sums as a product (multiplication) of their GCF and another sum.

a. The GCF of 27 and 72 is _____

$27x + 72 =$ ____ (____ + ____)

b. The GCF of 84 and 132 is _____

$84y + 132x =$ ____ (____ + ____)

4. A company held a business meeting and 15% of its employees arrived late. If 68 employees arrived on time, how many employees does the company have?

5. Divide using long division, and round the answers to three decimals.

   a. $0.614 \div 7$

   b. $178 \div 1.4$

6. Refer to the pictures and add.

a. $(-2) + 4 =$ _____

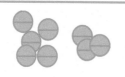

b. $(-5) + (-3) =$ _____

7. Write an addition sentence for the picture.

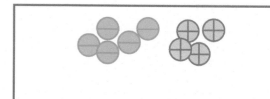

Skills Review 59

1. Write a subtraction sentence to match each picture.

a.

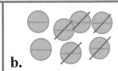

b.

2. Either change the decimal into a fraction, or vice versa. You decide which way is easier!
   Then, calculate mentally.

a. $0.7 + \dfrac{1}{5}$	**b.** $\dfrac{8}{20} - 0.35$	**c.** $\dfrac{3}{10} - 0.16$	**d.** $4.3 + 9\dfrac{3}{4}$

3. Draw a picture to illustrate the multiplication, and fill in.

   Total area: _8_ · (_3_ + _5_)

   The areas of the two rectangles:

   _____ · _____ and _____ · _____

4. Anna needed 3 cups of flour to make a batch of cookies.
   She found a bag that had 2 2/3 cups of flour, and another
   bag that had 2 1/8 cups of flour. How much flour did she
   have left after making the cookies?

5. Andrew can type 780 words in 12 minutes. How many
   words can he type in 15 minutes?

6. Find the least common multiple of the numbers using any method.

a. 14 and 21	**b.** 16 and 40

7. Simplify the expressions by adding and subtracting like terms.

a. $5x^4 - 3x + 6 + 7x^6$	**b.** $22a + 14y + 8a - 6y - 3$

Skills Review 60

1. Add or subtract.

a. $8 + (-12) =$ _____
b. $(-7) - 9 =$ _____
c. $(-5) + (-6) =$ _____

2. Solve. Think how many times the fraction goes into the whole number.

a. $7 \div \dfrac{1}{8} =$	**b.** $5 \div \dfrac{1}{3} =$
c. $9 \div \dfrac{1}{7} =$	**d.** $4 \div \dfrac{1}{9} =$

3. Each measurement has an error, either in the unit or in the decimal point. Correct them.

   a. Brad is 1.8 cm tall.   **b.** Mary's thumb is about 6.3 mm long.

   c. The car is 46.9 m long.   **d.** My notebook is 19 m wide.

4. Write in order from the smallest to the largest.

a. 3.407 34.07 3.047	**b.** 0.815 0.851 0.581

5. Multiply. Shade a rectangle in the grid to illustrate the multiplications.

 **a.** $\dfrac{3}{4} \cdot \dfrac{3}{7} =$	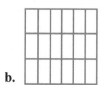 **b.** $\dfrac{2}{3} \cdot \dfrac{1}{6} =$	**c.** $\dfrac{1}{2} \cdot \dfrac{3}{4} =$

6. Kay took $150 with her when she went shopping. When she got done, she had $45 left. What percentage of the $150 did she spend?

7. Find the price for 3 ¼ pounds of dates if one pound costs $9.

8. Find the missing factor or divisor.

a. $2.48 \cdot$ _____ $= 24.8$ $5.729 \cdot$ _____ $= 572.9$	**b.** $\dfrac{63}{\rule{2cm}{0.4pt}} = 0.63$	**c.** $\dfrac{7.4}{\rule{2cm}{0.4pt}} = 0.0074$

Skills Review 61

1. Find the missing side length of the rectangles when one side and the area are given.

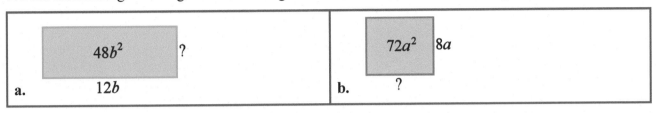

a. $48b^2$? $12b$

b. $72a^2$ $8a$?

2. The distances that Paul and Norman each drive to work are in a ratio of 2:3, respectively. Paul drives 24 ½ miles to work. How far does Norman drive?

3. Plot the points from the equation $y = x - 3$.

x	−6	−5	−4	−3	−2	−1	0	1
y	−9	−8	−7	−6	−5	−4	−3	−2

x	2	3	4	5	6	7	8	9
y	−1	0	1	2	3	4	5	6

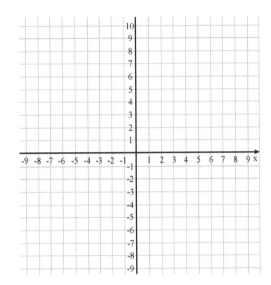

4. Write the equivalent rates.

a. $\dfrac{72 \text{ mi}}{4 \text{ hr}} = \dfrac{}{1 \text{ hr}} = \dfrac{}{30 \text{ min}} = \dfrac{}{20 \text{ min}}$

b. $\dfrac{\$8}{15 \text{ min}} = \dfrac{}{45 \text{ min}} = \dfrac{}{1 \text{ hr}} = \dfrac{}{1 \text{ hr } 30 \text{ min}}$

5. Divide using long division. Use a notebook. If the division is not even, give your answer to <u>three</u> decimal digits.

a. $0.5732 \div 0.6$

b. $9.4017 \div 0.0023$

c. $0.013 \div 0.02$

6. Find percentages of the quantities.

a. 60% of $7.50 _____

b. 75% of 8.2 m _____

c. 4% of 260 lb _____

Skills Review 62

1. Estimate the result using mental math and rounded numbers. Find the exact value using a calculator. Also, find the error of estimation.

> $297,428 - 12 \cdot 7,249$
>
> Estimation:
>
> Exact:
>
> Error of estimation:

2. Write the multiplications as expressions of a "percentage of the number".

a. $0.7 \cdot 30$ _____ % of _____ = _____
b. $0.09 \cdot \$600$ _____ % of _____ = _____
c. $0.05 \cdot 8$ _____ % of _____ = _____

3. Write in expanded form, as a sum.

   a. 0.732

   b. 0.005163

4. Find the aspect ratio of each rectangle:

   a. a rectangle whose height is 3/8 of its width

   b. a rectangle whose height is six times its width

5. Subtract or multiply the measuring units.

a.	b.
$\begin{array}{r} 80 \text{ ft} \quad 4 \text{ in} \\ - \ 26 \text{ ft} \quad 7 \text{ in} \\ \hline \end{array}$	$\begin{array}{r} 5 \text{ lb} \quad 9 \text{ oz} \\ \times \qquad\quad 6 \\ \hline \end{array}$

6. Draw a trapezoid with one 66° angle, where the base side is 8 cm long and the side parallel to the base is 4.4 cm long. Is there only one trapezoid like that, or could there be several different ones?

   (Hint: The instructions do not say where the 66° angle has to be, so you can choose!)

Skills Review 63

1. Draw a triangle that has a 25° angle, a 110° angle, and a 4″ side between those angles.

2. Divide. For each division, write a corresponding multiplication sentence.

a.	b.	c.	d.
$0.42 \div 7 =$	$6.3 \div 0.9 =$	$0.024 \div 4 =$	$0.35 \div 0.05 =$

3. *Estimate* the discounted price.

   a. 35% off of a $69 popcorn popper

   b. 18% off of a $364 laptop

4. Write as percentages, fractions, and decimals.

a. $120\% = \dfrac{}{} = $ _____	**b.** _____ $\% = \dfrac{409}{100} = $ _____	**c.** _____ $\% = \dfrac{}{} = 0.13$

5. Simplify before you multiply, or just simplify (in a).

a. $\dfrac{60}{85} =$	**b.** $\dfrac{36}{14} \cdot \dfrac{8}{20} =$	**c.** $\dfrac{54}{72} \cdot \dfrac{15}{48} =$

6. Write the numbers in order from the least to the greatest.

a. $-6 \quad 1 \quad -2 \quad 0$	**b.** $2 \quad -1 \quad 7 \quad -4$

Skills Review 64

1. Draw right triangles whose two perpendicular sides are given below, and then find their areas.

   a. 2.3 cm and 4 cm

   b. 3 ¼ inches and 1 ¾ inches

2. Write an equation, and find the part that is not given.

Statement	Equation
a. The quotient is 7, the divisor is 9, the dividend is _____.	_____ ÷ _____ = _____
b. The subtrahend is _____, the difference is 26, and the minuend is 81.	_____ − _____ = _____

3. Continue the sequences for six more numbers. Use mental math.

   a. 0.37, 0.44, 0.51,

   b. 4.165, 4.17, 4.175,

4. One brand of quadcopter drone costs $295, and another brand costs 3/5 of that price. Eric bought the more expensive quadcopter, and Mitch bought two of the cheaper ones. Who spent more money? How much more?

5. Lisa bought 6.1 *kilograms* of tomatoes. Maya bought 13 *pounds* of tomatoes. Whose tomatoes weighed more? (1 kg = 2.2 lb)

6. Identify the errors that these children made. Then find the correct answers.

a. Find 40% of 30.	**b.** Find 25% of 7,200.
Sonia's solution: 0.04 · 30 = 1.2	Harold's solution: This is the same as 7,200 ÷ 3 = 2,400.

Skills Review 65

1. Find the greatest common factor of the given numbers.

a. 36, 72, and 81	**b.** 48, 63, and 84

2. Draw an altitude to each parallelogram. Highlight or "thicken" the base. Then find the areas.

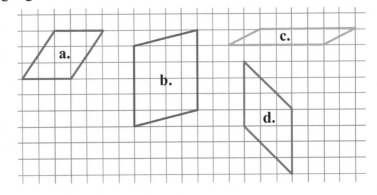

    a. _____ sq. units

    b. _____ sq. units

    c. _____ sq. units

    d. _____ sq. units

3. Find the root of the equation $x^2 + 27 - 4x = 59$ in the set $\{0, 1, 5, 8, 10\}$.

4. Round the decimals to the underlined place.

a. 0.51802$\underline{7}$14	**b.** 2$\underline{6}$.14918	**c.** 0.26$\underline{3}$5149

5. Mia gave away 40% of her stuffed animals and now she has 18 left. How many did she have originally?

6. Carla had 5/8 as much money as Hannah had.

    a. Draw a bar model to represent the situation.

    b. Hannah spent 1/4 of her money. Draw another bar model to represent the new situation.

    c. Carla has $120. How much money does Hannah have after spending 1/4 of her money?

7. Plot these inequalities on the number line.

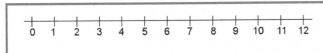

a. $x < 5$	**b.** $x \leq 33$

Skills Review 66

1. Draw as many different-shaped triangles as you can that each have an area of 9 square units.

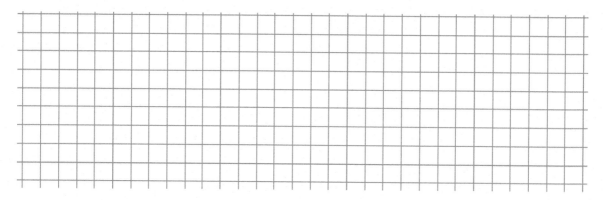

2. Write an expression. Solve.

   a. The difference of 7.4 and 3.9, multiplied by 5.

   b. First add 60 and 280, then divide the result by 4.

   c. The quantity 3 times 2, cubed.

3. Write an expression for the perimeter of each shape in simplified form.

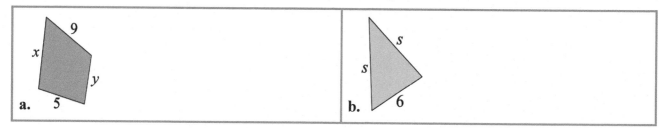

4. Write the decimals as fractions and multiply both.

a. $0.7 \cdot 0.06 =$	**b.** $0.005 \cdot 1.1 =$	**c.** $1.2 \cdot 0.0008 =$
↓ ↓ ↓	↓ ↓ ↓	↓ ↓ ↓

5. **a.** Draw a picture: There are squares and triangles, and the ratio of squares to all the shapes is 2:5.

   b. What is the ratio of squares to triangles?

6. **a.** Express the sum 35 + 50 as a product (multiplication), using the GCF of the numbers as the common factor.

b. Draw two rectangles, side by side, to represent the product you wrote.

7. Add or subtract the fractions.

a. $\dfrac{3}{7} + \dfrac{5}{8} + \dfrac{1}{2}$	**b.** $\dfrac{11}{12} - \dfrac{1}{2} - \dfrac{2}{9}$

Skills Review 67

1. This shape consists of a triangle and a parallelogram. Calculate its total area.

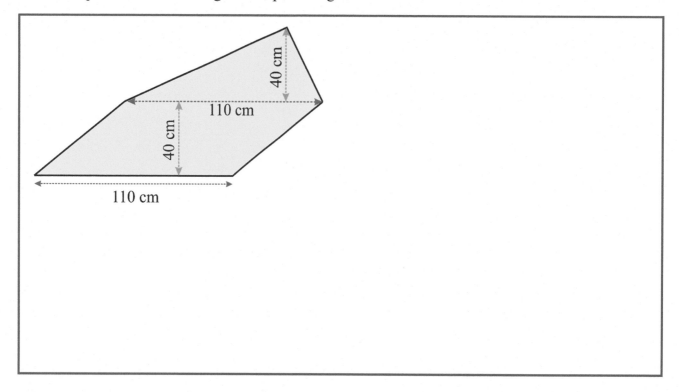

2. Change to unit rates. Give the rate using the word "per" or the slash / .

   a. Jared travels 1,625 miles in 25 hours.

   b. It costs $140 for 35 pounds of almonds.

3. **a.** Find four numbers that are multiples of both 7 and 5.
   What is the LCM of 7 and 5?

   b. Find four numbers that are multiples of both 3 and 8.
   What is the LCM of 3 and 8?

4. Find the missing number or variable in these area models.

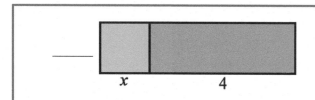

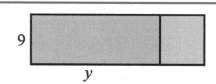

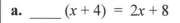

a. _____ $(x + 4) = 2x + 8$

b. The total area is $9y + 63$.

5. Find the distances between the points.

   a. (15, 32) and (15, −49)

   b. (−53, 21) and (−7, 21)

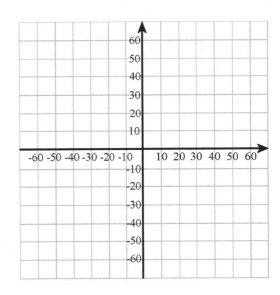

6. Marilyn and Marcella each had $50. Marilyn spent $20, and Marcella spent $35. What percentage of their money did each girl spend?

7. Divide using long division. If the division is not exact, round the answer to three decimals.

a. $0.716 \div 8$	**b.** $293 \div 12$

Skills Review 68

1. Multiply. Give your answers in lowest terms.

a. $\dfrac{5}{12} \cdot \dfrac{2}{9} \cdot \dfrac{1}{4}$	**b.** $3\dfrac{1}{5} \cdot 6\dfrac{7}{8}$

2. Draw any pentagon using grid points as vertices. Then find its area.

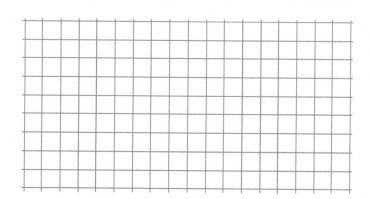

3. Joel has 5 meters of string. How many sections that are 0.3 of a meter long each can he cut from the string?

How long is the section of string that he has left?

4. Find the percentages. Use mental math.

a. 10% of 70 kg _____	**b.** 30% of $25 _____	**c.** 40% of 60 mi _____

5. Rewrite the expressions using an exponent, then solve them. You may use a calculator.

  a. $7 \cdot 7 \cdot 7 \cdot 7 \cdot 7$

  b. 500 cubed

6. Justin lays an average of 150 blocks a day. Consider the variables time (t), measured in days, and number of blocks laid (b).

  a. Fill in the table.

  b. Plot the points on the coordinate grid.

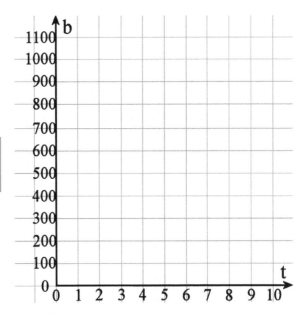

t (days)	1	2	3	4	5	6	7
b							

  c. Write an equation that relates b and t.

  d. Which of the two variables is the independent variable?

7. Use the given ratios to convert the measuring units. Round your answers to one decimal digit.

a. Use $1 = \dfrac{1.6093 \text{ km}}{1 \text{ mi}}$ to convert 7.3 mi to kilometers.

  7.3 mi =

b. Use $1 = \dfrac{0.946 \text{ L}}{1 \text{ qt}}$ to convert 9 qt to liters.

  9 qt =

Skills Review 69

1. Compare the numbers and write $<$, $=$, or $>$.

   a. 0.0003 ☐ 0.0000094   **b.** 49 thousandths ☐ 0.08   **c.** 0.000072 ☐ 72 millionths

2. **a.** Each bus (**b**) owned by a certain tour company has a
    capacity for 56 passengers (**p**). Fill in the table of rates.

p										
b	1	2	3	4	5	6	7	8	9	10

   b. Write an equation relating the number of buses (**b**) and the number of passengers (**p**).

3. Add.

a. $^-6 + ^-4 =$	**b.** $^-9 + 6 =$	**c.** $80 + (-30) =$

4. Write in normal form (as a number).

   $6 \times 10^3 + 4 \cdot 10^1 + 8 \cdot 10^5 =$

5. Solve. Remember to check to make sure your answer makes sense.

a. $\dfrac{2}{7} \div 6$	**b.** $\dfrac{7}{9} \div \dfrac{2}{11}$

6. Find the area and perimeter of this shape.

   Area =

   Perimeter =

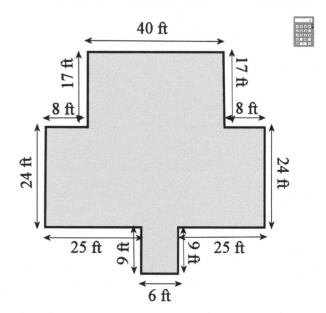

Skills Review 70

1. Identify the following quadrilaterals:

a. _____   b.  _____   c.  _____

2. The *volume* of a cube is 64 cubic feet.
   Find its surface area.

3. Find the distance between the two numbers. Then, write a matching subtraction sentence. To get a positive distance, remember to *subtract the <u>smaller</u> number from the <u>bigger</u> number.*

a. The distance between 7 and −12 is _____ .	**b.** The distance between −3 and −14 is _____ .
Subtraction: _____ − _____ = _____	Subtraction: _____ − _____ = _____

4. Joyce used 2/5 of her pay check to pay bills. Then, she loaned 1/4 of what was left of her pay check to her sister, and now she has $288 left. How much was Joyce's pay check originally?

5. Write as fractions and also as mixed numbers.

a. 209.2703	**b.** 4.05168

6. Multiply both the dividend and the divisor by 10, 100, or 1,000 to make a new division problem where the divisor is a whole number. Then divide.

a.	2.7	÷	0.09		
	_____	÷	_____	=	_____
b.	4.8	÷	0.6		
	_____	÷	_____	=	_____
c.	100	÷	0.005		
	_____	÷	_____	=	_____

7. Find the prime factorization of the number.

336

Skills Review 71

1. Draw a triangle that has a 67° angle,
   a 75° angle, and a 5-cm side between
   those angles.

2. Multiply or divide.

a. $2{,}600 \div 10{,}000 =$	**b.** $10^3 \cdot 0.020749 =$
c. $10^5 \cdot 52.3176 =$	**d.** $4.713 \div 1000 =$

3. **a.** Write an expression for the area of this shape.

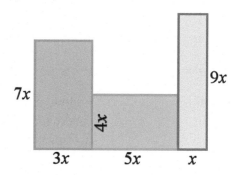

   b. Evaluate the expression if $x = 4$ cm.

   c. Evaluate the expression if $x = 8$ cm.

4. Imagine or sketch a rectangle with 5 ft and 9 ft sides.
   The area in square *feet* is _____ ft · _____ ft = _____ ft².

   The area in square *inches* is _____ in · _____ in = _____ in².

5. Find the missing integer.

a. $-6 +$ _____ $= -9$	**b.** $8 +$ _____ $= 0$	**c.** $10 -$ _____ $= -3$
$7 +$ _____ $= -5$	$-8 -$ _____ $= -2$	$6 +$ _____ $= 4$

6. Solve. Check each division with multiplication.

a. $\dfrac{5}{7} \div \dfrac{1}{4}$	**Check:**
b. $\dfrac{7}{8} \div \dfrac{3}{5}$	**Check:**
c. $1\dfrac{4}{5} \div \dfrac{2}{9}$	**Check:**

Skills Review 72

1. Divide using long division. Use a notebook. If the division is not even, give your answer to <u>two</u> decimal digits.

a. $78 \div 0.04$	**b.** $1.05 \div 1.8$

2. Make up your own rules, and then plot the points using the number pairs.

	x					
	y					

	x					
	y					

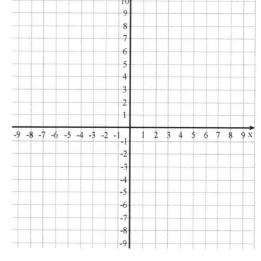

3. A rectangular swimming pool is four times as long as it is wide.

   a. What is its aspect ratio?

   b. The perimeter of the pool is 120 ft.
      Find its width and length.

   c. Find its area.

4. Divide in parts, then add or subtract the results.

a. $\dfrac{5{,}200 - 80}{5}$	**b.** $\dfrac{360 + 27 - 9}{9}$	**c.** $\dfrac{24 \text{ L } 300 \text{ ml}}{6}$

5. Find the areas of these compound shapes.

a.

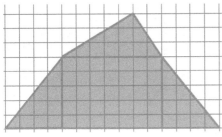

b.

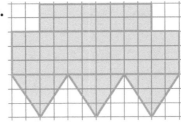

6. What is the total volume of these figures, in cubic units?

a. The edges of each little cube measure 1/2 in.

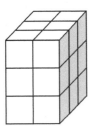

width = _____ in

height = _____ in

depth = _____ in

_____ little cubes, each _1/8_ in³

V = _____

b. The edges of each little cube measure 1/3 in.

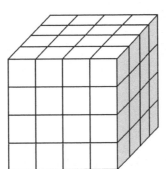

width = _____ in

height = _____ in

depth = _____ in

_____ little cubes, each _____ in³

V = _____

c. The edges of each little cube measure 1/4 in.

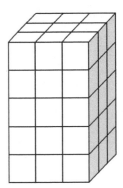

width = _____ in

height = _____ in

depth = _____ in

_____ little cubes, each _____ in³

V = _____

Skills Review 73

1. Calculate the volume of the toolbox
   on the right.

12 in

20.5 in

8.5 in

2. Write an expression for each situation.

   a. Four friends share the cost of a game that costs s dollars.
How much does each one pay?

   b. You bought m books at $9 each and n folders at $2.25 each.
What was the total cost?

3. Solve using mental math.

a. $240 + 3 \cdot 25$	**b.** $4{,}000 \div 10 - 500 \div 2$	**c.** $60 \cdot 70 - 30 \cdot 20$
=	=	=

4. A display of fruit contains oranges, grapefruit, and lemons in a ratio of 5:2:4, respectively.

   a. Draw a bar model to represent the situation.

   b. What is the ratio of lemons to the total number
of pieces of fruit?

   c. If there are 264 pieces of fruit in total, how many
grapefruit are in the display?

5. Write the amounts with derived units (units with prefixes) and a single-digit number.

a. 4,000 g = ___4___ ___kg___	**b.** 0.7 m = _____ _____	**c.** 0.9 L = _____ _____
600 L = _____ _____	0.05 L = _____ _____	0.003 g = _____ _____

6. Find the number that is missing from the equations.

a. 7 − _____ = ⁻10	**b.** ⁻2 + _____ = 0	**c.** 0 − _____ = ⁻7	**d.** ⁻3 + _____ = 8

7. Draw as many differently-shaped parallelograms as you can that all have an area of 20 square units.

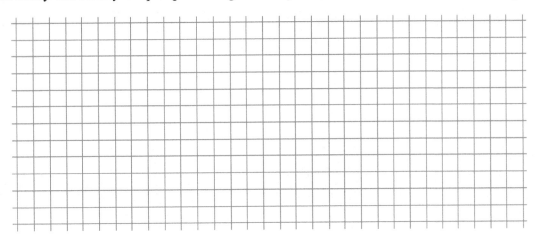

1. Write the numbers in order from the least to the greatest.

a. 3 −9 −12 0	**b.** 6 −7 8 −2

2. Find the area of this triangle in square centimeters. Round your final answer to the nearest whole square centimeter. (You will need to draw an altitude in the triangle.)

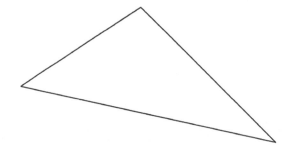

3. Make a dot plot from this data (the number of minutes that Kathy spent practicing the flute on weekdays during the month of February). You need to place a dot for each observation.

45 40 40 60 35 45 25 45 30 40
25 45 50 40 30 60 35 50 40 50

a. Describe the shape of the distribution.

b. Where is the peak of the distribution?

c. How many observations are there?

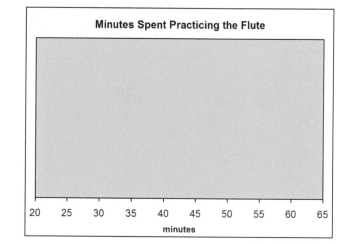

4. Find the greatest common factor of the given numbers.

a. 16, 40, and 120	**b.** 60, 75, and 135

5. Megan's neighbor had 35 plants for sale.
   Megan bought 40% of the plants.
   How many plants did she buy?

6. Add or subtract the fractions.

a. $\dfrac{7}{12} + \dfrac{5}{8} + \dfrac{1}{5}$	b. $\dfrac{5}{3} - \dfrac{1}{6} - \dfrac{1}{11}$

7. Write ratios of the given quantities. Use the fraction line to write the ratios. Then, simplify the ratios.
   You will need to *convert* one quantity so it has the same measuring unit as the other.

a. 7 cups and 5 pints	b. 600 m and 2.8 km

Skills Review 75

1. Find the median and mode of these data sets.

   a. 18, 22, 17, 25, 18, 20, 25, 18, 20, 15, 18, 22 (prices of shirts that Ken and Alex bought)

   median _____   mode _____

   b. brown, blue, green, brown, blue, brown, blue, brown (eye colors of a group of friends)

   mode _____

2. Divide this quadrilateral into triangles, and then find its area in square centimeters (to the nearest square centimeter). You may use a calculator.

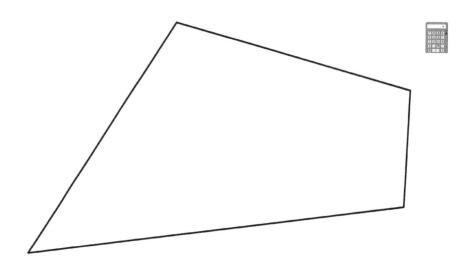

3. Make equivalent fractions by multiplying the given fraction by different forms of the number 1.

a. Multiply the fraction by $\frac{7}{7}$.	**b.** Multiply the fraction by $\frac{4}{4}$.	**c.** Multiply the fraction by $\frac{9}{9}$.
$\rule{0.6cm}{0.01cm} \cdot \frac{4}{5} =$	$\rule{0.6cm}{0.01cm} \cdot \frac{7}{8} =$	$\rule{0.6cm}{0.01cm} \cdot \frac{5}{11} =$

4. It took Randall three hours to read 105 pages of a book. If he continues reading at the same speed, how many pages will he have read in seven hours?

5. Abby drew a secret figure, and then she moved it 6 units down. The vertices of the moved figure are now at: (−5, −4), (2, −2), (6, −4), and (−4, −8). What were the coordinates of the original vertices?

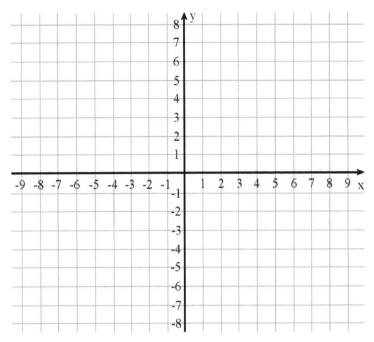

6. Find the percentages. Use mental math.

| **a.** 30% of 50 kg _____ | **b.** 10% of $25 _____ | **c.** 60% of 45 mi _____ |

7. Lauren bought a blouse for $14.20, pants for $22.95, shoes for $31.80, and two skirts for $8 each.

a. Estimate the total cost by rounding the numbers.

b. Find the exact cost and the error of estimation.

Skills Review 76

1.

a. Classify this triangle according to its sides and angles.

b. Reflect it in the *y*-axis.

c. Find its area.

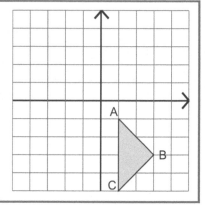

2. For the following data set:

- Create a dot plot.
- Name your graph.
- Indicate how many observations there are.

- Does this distribution have large, medium, or little spread?
- Choose measure(s) of center that describe the peak of the distribution, and calculate them.

Students' test scores in a history test:

70 72 75 90 85 90 95 100 85 100 75 85 100 72 85
68 85 70 95 100 72 80 75 90 84 92 95 75 70 85

3. Multiply.

a. $90 \cdot 0.06 \cdot 0.002 =$	**b.** $50 \cdot 0.3 \cdot 0.007 =$

4. Rewrite these sentences using symbols, and solve the resulting sums.

   a. The sum of eight positives and six negatives.

   b. Add −5 and −12.

   c. Positive 50 and negative 13 added together.

5. Find the reciprocal numbers. Then write a multiplication with the given number and its reciprocal.

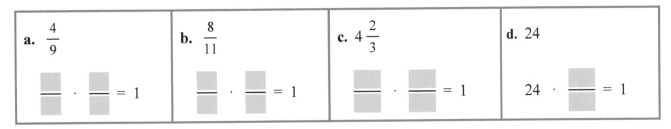

a. $\dfrac{4}{9}$	**b.** $\dfrac{8}{11}$	**c.** $4\dfrac{2}{3}$	**d.** 24

6. Write the equivalent rates.

a. $\dfrac{3 \text{ in}}{9 \text{ ft}} = \dfrac{}{3 \text{ ft}} = \dfrac{}{15 \text{ ft}} = \dfrac{}{21 \text{ ft}}$	**b.** $\dfrac{\$6}{15 \text{ min}} = \dfrac{}{5 \text{ min}} = \dfrac{}{40 \text{ min}} = \dfrac{}{1 \text{ hr } 20 \text{ min}}$

7. Find the least common multiple of the numbers using any method.

a. 18 and 27	**b.** 60 and 75

1. Draw a number line jump for each problem.

   a. $-9 + 4 =$ _____   **b.** $0 - 6 =$ _____

2. A picture frame is 4/5 as wide as it is high.

   a. What is its aspect ratio?

   b. The picture frame's perimeter is 72 in.
   What is its area?

3. Find the range and the interquartile range of the data set.

The weights of some baby rabbits in grams:

   34 35 35 35 35 36 37 37 37 38 39 40 40 40 41

   range _____

   1st quartile _____   median _____   3rd quartile _____

   interquartile range _____

4. On paper, Mr. Brown's plan for a shed
   measures $7'' \cdot 16''$. In reality, the shed
   is 24 times as big. Find the perimeter of
   the shed in feet and its area in square feet.

5. Mom is making granola for a camping trip.
   She wants to make enough for 40 servings.
   Calculate the amount of each ingredient
   she needs.

Granola – 16 servings
1/2 cup of coconut sugar
1/2 cup of molasses
1/4 cup of coconut oil
4 cups of oats
1/2 tsp of cinnamon
1/4 tsp of salt

6. Simplify, or simplify and multiply.

   a. $\dfrac{36}{144} =$

   b. $\dfrac{12}{35} \cdot \dfrac{14}{64} =$

7. Write the multiplications as expressions
   of a "percentage of the number".

   a. $0.4 \cdot 90$

   _____ % of _____ = _____

   b. $0.08 \cdot \$300$

   _____ % of _____ = _____

Skills Review 78

1. Draw a net for each of these rectangular prisms.

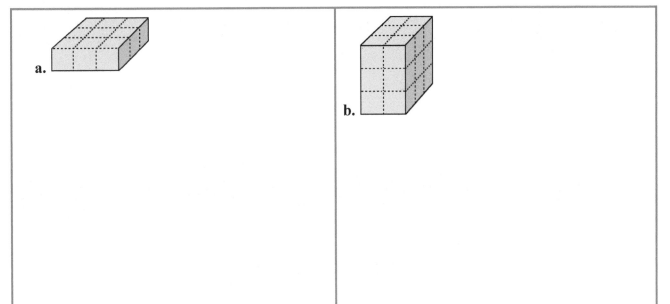

2. Measure the figures and find their areas in square millimeters and in square centimeters. Round the area in square millimeters to the nearest ten square millimeters, and the area in square centimeters to the nearest tenth of a square centimeter.

a. _____ mm^2 **b.** _____ mm^2 **c.** _____ mm^2

_____ cm^2 _____ cm^2 _____ cm^2

3. *Estimate* the discounted price.

   a. 40% off of a $48.90 blender

   b. 18% off of a $15.50 pair of sandals

4. Solve.

a. $-6 - (-8) =$	**b.** $2 - (-7) =$	**c.** $-18 + 13 =$
$4 + (-9) =$	$3 - 5 =$	$-16 - 10 =$

5. Solve the equations.

| **a.** $6x = \dfrac{3}{5}$ | **b.** $4x = \dfrac{1}{2}$ |

6. This data lists the prices of 26 different books in dollars. Make a histogram with <u>four</u> bins.

9   12   14   14   15   15   16   17   17   18   19   19   19
20   20   21   24   25   25   26   27   28   29   33   35   37

Price ($)	Frequency

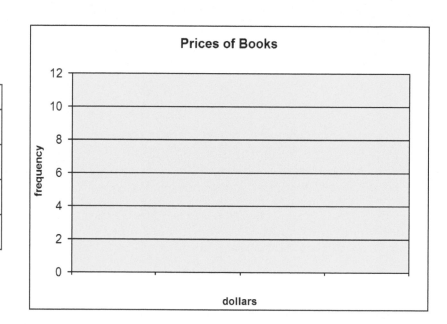

7. Use mental math to fill in the missing numbers:

a. Of 70 children, 14 are girls.	**b.** Out of 150 buttons, 60% are red.
_____% of the children are girls.	So, _____ of the buttons are red.

Skills Review 79

1. The price of a motorcycle was discounted by 20% and now it costs $8,000. What was the original price?

2. Make the five-number summary for the data set, and draw a boxplot. Hint: For the boxplot, first draw a number line with an appropriate range.

   the number of hours that Jacob spent exercising each month for a year

   15 15 16 17 17 18 20 21 21 21 25 25

   minimum

   1st quartile

   median

   3rd quartile

   maximum

3. Show that the volume of a box that measures 2 2/3 in. by 1 in. by 1 1/3 in. is indeed

$$V = \frac{8}{3} \text{ in} \cdot 1 \text{ in} \cdot \frac{4}{3} \text{ in} = \frac{32}{9} \text{ in}^3.$$

   How?

   (i)   Build a physical model *or* draw a sketch of the box, using 1/3 in. by 1/3 in. by 1/3 in. little cubes.

   (ii) Count the number of little cubes needed.

   (iii) Multiply the number of little cubes by the volume of ONE little cube.

4. Add or subtract.

a. $-5 + 9 =$ _____ $-2 - (-8) =$ _____	b. $(-6) - 10 =$ _____ $-4 + (-3) =$ _____	c. $-12 - 7 =$ _____ $(-9) + (-12) =$ _____

5. Gwen had 4/6 as many stickers as Beth. Then, Beth gave 15 of her stickers to Gwen, and now they both have the same amount of stickers. How many stickers did Beth have originally?

   Hint: Drawing a bar model can help.

6. Divide using long division. Round the answers to three decimals.

a. $318.7 \div 19$	b. $43 \div 8$

Skills Review 80

1. First find the GCF of the numbers. Then factor the expressions using the GCF.

a. GCF of 18 and 26 is _____ 18 + 26 = ____ (____ + ____)	**b.** GCF of 45 and 75 is _____ 45 + 75 = ____ (____ + ____)

2. The gift box on the right measures 40 cm by 20 cm by 12 cm.

   a. Calculate its volume.

   b. (Challenge) Angela bought some homemade bars of soap that measured 8 cm by 5 cm by 3 cm. She fit as many bars in the box as possible, and she was able to do that without leaving any gaps. How many bars of soap did she fit in the box?

3. Find the percentages. Use mental math.

a. 25% of 60 kg _____	**b.** 75% of $28 _____	**c.** 90% of 40 mi _____

4. **a.** Write the points from the graph in the table.

x							
y							

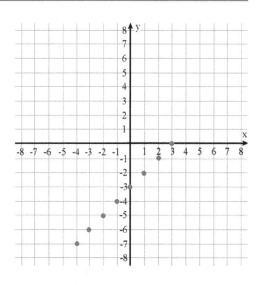

   b. Find the pattern the x- and y-coordinates follow in (a), and use that same pattern to fill in the table below.

x	4	5	6	7	8
y					

5. First change the fractions to decimals. Then calculate.

a. $\dfrac{3}{10} + \dfrac{426}{10{,}000} - \dfrac{39}{1{,}000}$

b. $\dfrac{74}{100} + \dfrac{17}{10{,}000} - \dfrac{1}{4}$

6. **a.** Complete the stem-and-leaf plot for this data. This time, the stem is the first two digits of the numbers, and the leaves are the last digits.

   543 548 563 569 571 579 586 594 597 615 622 638

   (weekly cost of groceries over a 12-week-period, in dollars, for the Hill family)

   b. Find the median weekly cost of groceries.

   c. Find the interquartile range.

   d. Describe the spread of the distribution
   (is the data spread out a lot, a medium amount, a little, *etc.*)

Stem	Leaf

   54 | 3 means 543

7. Use the given ratios to convert the measuring units. Round your answers to one decimal digit.

a. Use $1 = \dfrac{2.54 \text{ cm}}{1 \text{ in}}$ to convert 67 inches to centimeters.	
67 in =	
b. Use $1 = \dfrac{0.454 \text{ kg}}{1 \text{ lb}}$ to convert 28 pounds to kilograms.	
28 lb =	